How to Fix Northern Ireland

By the same author

Non-fiction

The Trouble with Guns

I Was a Teenage Catholic

The Telling Year

Empty Pulpits

Under His Roof

On My Own Two Wheels

Gerry Adams: An Unauthorised Life

Fifty Years On: The Troubles and the Struggle for Change in Northern Ireland

The Year of Chaos: Northern Ireland on the Brink of Civil War, 1971–72

Can Ireland Be One?

Fiction

Terry Brankin Has a Gun

How to Fix Northern Ireland

Malachi O'Doherty

Atlantic Books
London

First published in hardback in Great Britain in 2023 by
Atlantic Books, an imprint of Atlantic Books Ltd.

10 9 8 7 6 5 4 3 2 1

A CIP catalogue record for this book is available
from the British Library.

Trade paperback ISBN: 978-1-83895-852-7
E-book ISBN: 978-1-83895-853-4

Printed in Great Britain by TJ Books Limited.

Atlantic Books
An imprint of Atlantic Books Ltd
Ormond House
26–27 Boswell Street
London
WC1N 3JZ

www.atlantic-books.co.uk

MIX
Paper from
responsible sources
FSC   FSC® C013056
www.fsc.org

For Maureen

Falkirk Council	
30124 03181216 9	
Askews & Holts	
941.6082	£16.99
MK	

Contents

A Note on the Text

In this book I have departed from the customary use of upper case for reference to religious designation, as in Protestant, Catholic etc. I use lower case with reference to catholic schools, catholic people, protestant streets, etc. I retain the upper case for references to the institutional churches and to the ideologies, e.g. the Presbyterian Church, Protestantism, etc.

My logic is that the upper case for a catholic man implies a respect for the fact of him being a catholic, whereas his being catholic – his Catholicism – may be no more significant in his life than his being a footballer or a husband, neither of which would normally be upper case. And these terms are used so much in this book that I think that typographically the ubiquity of the upper case is inelegant.

Prologue

It was the day of the referendum on the Good Friday Agreement.

That agreement, six weeks earlier, had been celebrated as an historic breakthrough bringing peace to Northern Ireland after thirty years of violence. The world saw Northern Ireland's trouble as some kind of confused religious war, a relic of religious wars in Europe which had ended four hundred years before. In part it was. Weren't the Irish nationalists catholics and the British unionists protestants? Was that not centrally important?

The naming of the agreement after that holy day on which it had been completed seemed also to recognise that religion was at the heart of the inter-communal dispute and carried a suggestion that a spiritual breakthrough had occurred around the central fact cherished in both communities, that Christ had died for peace.

For the poetically minded and the devout that suggestion might have impressed. It echoed and perhaps finalised an earlier reference to Easter in the marking of historic Irish days, the Easter Rising of 1916.

The agreement, however, was not poetic. It was the opposite. It had sought to encapsulate long-simmering passions as hard realities and to seek a contractual agreement between bitter factions. It did this at first by paying respect to the forces that had contended with each other historically, acknowledged that each had a legitimate case, a grievance inherited from a troubled past. It classed the violence as political and prescribed a political solution. The problem was not that protestants were evil bigots contemptuous of the Catholic Church and Gaelic culture; nor was it that the catholics were slaves to a foreign church and besotted with blood-drenched mythologies. Neither was it that Britain was a voracious imperial despoiler of Irish decency. All of these analyses were freely available and routinely expressed.

The framers of the Good Friday Agreement, signed on 10 April 1998, chose to describe the past decades of bloodshed, terror and mayhem as a political conflict. At its heart was the question of whether Northern Ireland was British or Irish. Sort that out, they decided, and peace and good relations would follow. The past was indeed part of the problem.

Most of the island of Ireland had taken a road to progressive independence from Britain after a guerrilla war nearly eighty years earlier but six counties in the North had stayed within the United Kingdom.

For decades, the Irish Republican Army (IRA) had been campaigning for British withdrawal through bombing and murder. The British would probably have left if they could, but most of the people in Northern Ireland were British themselves and could not simply be dumped. The British army had entered the territory in force to suppress resistance. Armed protestant loyalist factions had sought to aid them by sending death squads out to murder random catholics and, when they could get them, members of the IRA.

This had all been messy and bloody and unpopular but seemed, decade after decade, to be going nowhere, without anyone having any idea of how to bring it to an end.

Animosities were encapsulated in song and daubed on the walls in graffiti and murals, some of them indeed quite artful. The level of violence, by the end of the seventies, had settled down to a routine average of a hundred murders a year. If there is a mistake at the heart of the agreement, it is in the presumption that all this was the work of reasonable people with intelligible grievances.

Murder was a crime, but political murder was a different category of crime and warranted early release once the political problem was resolved, so in the following two years the killers would go home. Some truly grotesque murders would be more or less absolved on the understanding that the motivation behind them had been removed by the agreement.

There was practical good sense behind that decision, for the paramilitary organisations had mobilised support around sympathy for the prisoners and had set up structures to raise funds for them and to campaign on their behalf. It was better to just let them all out to facilitate the dismantling of those structures rather than leave republican and loyalist groups with grievances and excuses.

Numerous books about the Northern Irish Troubles, up to that time, had ended with the conclusion that no obvious solution was in sight, the two communities being so resistant to integration with each other. The agreement, by contrast with this routine pessimism, was elegant and optimistic. It provided for a local power sharing assembly, run by Irish nationalists and pro-British unionists in partnership with each other. It set up cross-border institutions to involve the Irish government and provided for institutional connections between the governments of Britain and Ireland. All of this was to be enshrined in international treaty.

This was the three-stranded approach, the product of sophisticated diplomatic creativity and years of negotiation. Here was proof that a doggedly intractable conflict, often compared to the Israel–Palestine conflict, could be solved. This offered the whole world an example in creative peace-making.

The British and Irish diplomats were proud of what they had done. They had brought nationalist and unionist politicians to the table alongside their extreme and violent rivals within their own communities, and got them to accept a new formula for governing the region acceptable to most, if not all, political parties.

Naturally, everyone was happy. There were high hopes for the agreement's endorsement in a referendum. The world's media was in Belfast. I was a reporter working with a camera crew to make a little film about how people on the street felt about the breakthrough. This is what broadcasters wanted, not the close analysis of diplomatic and constitutional formulae but eager hopeful young people looking to a bright future.

We had found a smart young lad from east Belfast and we thought we would take him to one of the big loyalist political murals on the Newtownards Road and interview him there. The mural, black lettering on a white wall, declared: 'The Conflict is about Nationality'.

Well, that was pretty much the central point of the new agreement: two legitimate conceptions of nationality were to be accommodated within the one region.

We stood Tommy at the wall and prepared to set up the camera. This involved carrying the camera and the tripod from the car boot, setting up the camera and connecting it to the microphone managed by the sound guy. These things always took a little time, time for us to draw attention to ourselves.

The camera operator would want to check the white balance so that the painted wall would not have a blue or yellow hue. The producer would want to be sure that the picture was well framed and the sound guy would want to take levels from me and from Tommy to be sure that we came out on the tape – yes, actual tape in those days – without one of us sounding louder than the other. There was also the worry about the noise from passing traffic.

It was a nice sunny day. Men sitting outside a pub across the road were drinking pints and watching us intently. That was normal when you were filming outside. But what's this? They are coming over?

'What the fuck's going on here?' said the first to reach us, a hefty but smallish man in a green T-shirt that was stretched around his paunch. 'What's your name?' he said to Tommy. 'Speak up or we'll burn your fucking car.'

His friends had now joined us, three of them. One of them rested his arm across the camera to be sure that no one touched it.

I said, 'We are making a small film.'

'Who the fuck's talking to you? What's your name?'

There is something of which you will be aware if you are a Malachi, or Eamon or Seamus or Sean, and that is that your name declares that you are Irish, most likely catholic and therefore almost certainly a nationalist. Such a name will be treated as a declaration of affiliation even though your mother gave it to you before you got the vote, about eighteen years before you got the vote in fact. Nothing in the Good Friday Agreement was going to change that.

These guys, I was assuming, with my similar familiarity with the codes, were protestant loyalists. Their affiliation was to organisations which had killed people for having names like mine.

'What's your film about?'

'We're just sounding out people on what they think of the agreement and their hopes for the future.'

'You think everybody around here is behind this agreement, don't you? Well, you've another fucking think coming.'

I wasn't sure that getting into a political argument with him was the way to resolve this. At that point another man came round the corner to join us. I recognised him and he recognised me. He was a senior loyalist but of a type that had emerged during the political negotiations, mannered and conscientious. His value was in the respect he got from the hard men and his ability to translate their concerns into language that sounded astute and reasonable in a television interview.

He didn't say things like: 'Shut the fuck up.'

'Och, Malachi, it's you.'

This was a relief. This would get sorted out now.

'People are just a bit touchy with a camera around, and the lads just across the road having a drink want to be sure you're not filming them. And to tell you the truth, we don't want the impression to go out that the whole area is behind the agreement.'

The political party which represented these goons, and of which this man was a member, had actually helped negotiate the agreement.

'It's what you'd call nuanced, Malachi.'

He nodded to the hard men and they turned and went back across the road to their drinks.

'We'll go somewhere else,' said the producer, signalling to the camera operator and the sound guy to pack up, resting a reassuring hand on Tommy's shoulder.

Then this senior loyalist took me aside. He said, 'I'm very impressed by your work, Malachi. That film about the Christian Brothers.'

Really?

I had featured in a television documentary about the Irish Christian Brothers, a teaching order, accusing them of strident Gaelic chauvinism and, among other things, being too eager to use the cane or strap, and religious fundamentalism.

'That was noticed here. That went down well.'

And I suddenly realised what his point was. I had endorsed protestant perceptions of the Catholic Church as part of the problem. That made me an ally in the cause. And it wasn't the cause of national sovereignty. It wasn't something covered by the agreement that we were all voting on that day.

Religion was in the mix. In the streets in protestant areas the Catholic Church was still reviled as the enemy. Nothing in the agreement was designed to assuage that.

Had I not been there, this smoother-talking loyalist might have calmed down the thugs and saved the car and the camera. Or we might have lost both, and wee Tommy might have taken a kicking. Who knows how animosities are placated and what really makes the difference when tensions are high and brutes like the man in the green T-shirt are raging and ready?

Or that what eases the tension today will work in the same way tomorrow?

I went away from there wondering what faith we could really have in the agreement after all. Its creative diplomacy relied on an analysis of the problem which didn't take account of naive religious prejudice and the thrill of taking power on the street.

The best hope was that the agreement would be an enduring fix for an old problem. Failing that, at least protestant unionists and catholic nationalists would work together in the future, come to empathise more with each other and find a common interest in partnership. That hope has not been realised.

We need a new approach.

1

Where the Streets are Green and Orange

Let me take you for a dander round Belfast, my home city. We'll start from my front door.

This is a nice tree-lined street. The houses are in redbrick terraces, all much the same, three storeys high with sloping tiled roofs. You couldn't tell from the architecture that this isn't a part of Leeds or Liverpool. Nothing here is distinctly Belfast until you get to the end of the street and a clear view of the hills.

But let's walk. You will notice that every house has a car. There are no small children and that tells you something. This is a street for middle-aged professionals and retired people who own their houses. And people who own houses don't throw stones.

There is no graffiti on the walls. In the heat of summer, resin drips from the trees onto the cars. This sticky stuff holds the dust that blows in and is a bugger to scrub off. Middle-class problems. This is a nice place.

When I walk up the street towards the main road and the shops I often stop to talk to a neighbour, Jean who is an artist, Madge who has just had a new hip, Conor the academic lawyer, Maurice who has some kind of social services job, Eileen the retired journalist who has a weekly column.

I don't think there are any former paramilitaries in my street, orangemen or members of the security services. The window cleaner who comes once a week tells me he went to school with some loyalists. No one here puts out flags. There are no murals on gable walls. I don't think there is anything here that would tell a stranger whether the street was more catholic or protestant. I don't know. I don't go round asking people. They don't ask me but they don't have to. They can tell by my name, but you can't do that with everybody. Andy Burns over there cutting his hedge could be either with a name like that.

I know Morgan across the street is a presbyterian, active in a big church on the corner. The location of that church suggests this neighbourhood was once mainly protestant. There is also a church of Ireland church and a methodist church between here and the nearest catholic church. Amelia, further along, was married to a policeman who died.

This is not a typical street. If I threw a dart at a map of Belfast it would probably land on a street where people do put out flags, or do have graffiti, or where a tattooed ex-paramilitary prisoner walking his dog is known to everybody. I suppose the difference is class. I live in a middle-class street. Back in the nineties, when I moved in, a young professional couple would have been able to get a mortgage on a house like ours; not now. People who have been here a long time are not rich. New arrivals moving in … well, I can't think of any.

I feel safe in this street. I did not feel safe in the street I lived in as a young man, on a west Belfast housing estate, back in the seventies, where bombers mixed their ingredients in garden sheds and coaxed neighbours into minding guns for them. I doubt this street was ever barricaded.

There has been some trouble here. In the nineties I would lie in bed and listen to the commotion of protest and riot not far away. One night it came close. There was an incident when a car struck a stone gate post. Then there was the year the loyalists came up and painted the kerb stones red, white and blue. They still erect flags out there but you get used to them.

Once the police intercepted an armed IRA team near a school opposite the end of the street.

Charlie the taxi driver was shot dead by loyalists as he sat in his car round the corner waiting for business. The following night I didn't tell my wife that I was afraid to go across the road for a bottle of wine because I didn't want to make the fear palpable inside our home. So I went and got the wine.

But that was then.

Let's go out onto the main road now. Anything distinctly Belfast yet?

There is a steady flow of traffic into and out of town. On the other side of the road there is a Tesco and an Indian restaurant. From the lamp post outside a tanning salon hangs a large Union flag. That flag is fresh out of its packaging and you can still see the fold-lines in squares. If you can look at it with neutral eyes, you may think it adds a touch of festive colour to an otherwise ordinary road. But who here has neutral eyes?

July is coming, the season of parades and bonfires. It will start with marking the anniversary of the battle of the Somme, in which thousands of our grand-uncles and grandfathers were cut to ribbons by machine gun fire in muddy French fields. Protestants commemorate their losses there as proof of their loyalty to Britain. I don't know what they think other people's losses were proof of. But they take it very seriously. That large redbrick building with the flag, up there on the right, that's the Orange Hall and in front of it are black marble memorial stones to the dead of past wars.

If you had been here yesterday you would have seen the orangemen gather there and march down the road with their bands, a police car leading the way. They were a strange mix of sober dignity and ribaldry, the men in suits and orange collarettes marching proudly, the pipers playing martial tunes, the drummer beating the goatskin as if it was the head of someone he found objectionable.

Across the street at the bus stop a little girl practises her Irish dance steps as she waits with her mother. In the past, her mother would have stopped her drawing attention to herself. This dancing declares that she is Irish and catholic; or at least the lesser-informed loyalist – the worst kind – would take it as such. Cultural barriers are softening and some protestant children now learn Irish dancing and some protestants are learning the Irish language in east Belfast.

We'll walk towards the bridge across the river. The park is on our right with its grand trees and richly ornate flowerbeds, some of them at eye level above the grey stone wall. That park has history. In the early seventies the militaristic Ulster Vanguard rallied there and men in ranks were inspected like soldiers on parade and told to prepare for war.

I like the park. Now you are likely to hear Bengali or Polish spoken by people strolling by. The streets on the other side of the park form a more definable area than those on this side. That is a working-class protestant area and young men and women from there walk their dogs or exercise here. Sometimes the police drive along slowly, looking for drug dealers. Occasionally you will see a hungry-looking young man shudder and scowl as he walks, apparently doubting that he belongs here.

Not every passing jeer has a sectarian motive.

The main gate is flanked by sandstone pillars and bears the crest of the city.

I suspect few study that image, assuming it to be the lion and the unicorn contending for a shield. Actually the creature on the left looks like a wild dog with a chain round its neck and the one on the right is a winged creature with the head of a horse and the tail of a fish. Two creatures of different species apparently rage at each other, the one hampered by chains, the other by a hybrid biology; the one real and familiar, the mad dog, the other purely mythical, the flying seahorse.

The dog is a wolf or, some say, an Irish wolfhound, shackled, the crown for a collar. It has been tamed by British monarchy.

The seahorse also wears a crown around its neck, a different kind of crown suggestive of castellation, protection. So Britain, by this symbol, protects the gentle seahorse while taming the rabid Irish dog.

The shield itself depicts a ship at full sail, symbolising trade and military power with a global reach. In one corner is a bell held fast. This is not a pun that suggests the creators of the image knew their stuff. The 'bel' in Belfast is not a bell at all but derives from the Irish 'beal' meaning 'mouth', in this case the mouth of a river, probably the Farset which now flows under High Street and into the lough through a pipe lined with mussels and grime.

And the motto, '*Pro Tanto Quid Retribuamus*', is extracted from Psalm 116:12: 'What shall I render unto the Lord for all his benefits towards me?' The Lord has been removed from the line and, by implication, replaced with Britain.

This is blasphemy but the devout burghers seem never to have noticed.

Now we are at the River Lagan, a mile from where it opens out into the estuary, Belfast Lough. Here we are closer to the university and more likely to see the rowers from the boat club slicing through the water, puffing at their oars, a cyclist with a loudhailer following them along the embankment and shouting encouragement or instructions.

When the Orange Order parades down here with martial bands in July it must not cross this bridge. For years there were protests against the local lodge continuing by the direct route into the centre of town so now it must divert. That decision was based on an understanding that the people in the narrow streets beyond the river were catholics. From among them, protests had been organised against the parades. Bandsmen on the parades replied with jeering, and a determination was made that the bands and those people were best kept apart.

Across the road you will see the smaller terrace houses of the Holy Land where streets are named after Palestine, Jerusalem, Carmel, probably more in commemoration of British military campaigns than for their biblical connotations. This square mile was a working-class residential area, but now the houses are occupied by students, mostly catholic. When a band passed here recently a young man threw his food recycling bin at them and band members charged at the house but he dashed back in and shut the door.

The catholic students are usually on holiday when the bands pass through. Protestant students prefer to go to Scotland or England to study.

There are often flags on the lamp posts here, Irish tricolours, the green, white and orange. You'll see some young people in the green and white jersey of Glasgow Celtic. They support a Scottish football team but fly the Irish flag. It's all part of the one tradition to them.

In protestant areas you will see the Scottish flag, the Saltire. Young people there, somewhat less anomalously since they declare themselves to be British, support Glasgow Rangers.

You should see these streets on St Patrick's Day. Then the whole area is festive with hundreds of students dressed in green, partying from morning to night.

That pub, the Rose and Crown, might strike you as strangely named for a local in a catholic Irish area where tricolours fly. Six catholics died there when the Ulster Volunteer Force (UVF) threw a bomb in one night in February 1974. Many pubs and street corners in Belfast have stories like that. That bomb was an assertion of the right of Northern Ireland to be British at a time when people feared that the political advantage was flowing to those who were also throwing bombs in assertion of the right to be Irish.

We'll carry on past where the old gasworks was, now the setting of a fancy hotel, and towards the Markets area, which is not as vibrant as it once was. Places change character here.

When I was young you would still have seen the occasional horse and cart in the Markets, or the ragman. He even came out to the suburbs calling, 'Regs. Any regs!'

This is all a catholic area by the river. Some of the old streets have been redeveloped and a big civil service office building overshadows the old church, St Malachy's. When it was being built I reported on a campaign to stop it and to let the church continue to preside over the area as the predominant defining feature. As some consolation Prince Charles came to inspect the ornate white marble renovation of the altar. I covered that event too. The first minister and Democratic Unionist Party (DUP) leader Peter Robinson also came.

It is hard to comprehend the Belfast catholic attitude to royalty. Many catholics hold it only in contempt but the church was honoured to be visited by the future king. No doubt the bishop discussed architecture with him. Even IRA leaders have enjoyed the attention of royalty since then. Republicanism, in theory, is the total rejection of monarchy but theory doesn't determine how people respond to each other when they meet.

And there is the Albert Bridge over the Lagan. It is named after Prince Albert, just as the Royal Albert Hall in London is. I don't recall anyone ever raising a protest against that, or against Queen's Bridge further along, but as a teenager I was aware of a plan to name a new bridge after Sir Edward Carson, the leader of the campaign against home rule for Ireland, perhaps better known now for prosecuting the case against Oscar Wilde. Local nationalists were outraged and one protester even dropped a brick on the queen's car on a 1966 visit to Belfast.

Over the river is Short Strand, another catholic area, and then beyond that the population is mostly protestant, all the way out along the Newtownards Road. Even in recent years there has been sectarian rioting around Short Strand. In my youth we used to fear that this little catholic enclave would one day be overwhelmed by the vast surrounding protestant population, but it turns out that most of those people had no malign intent.

Further out, beyond the little houses built for protestant workers in the shipyard and the rope works, there is Ballyhackamore with the arts centre and nice cafes, coffee shops and bigger houses. It appears to take its name from the mud flats or sewage exposed in the lough at low tide. 'Bally' (baile) means 'town'. 'Hack' appears to come from the Irish word 'cac' for 'shit', and 'more' (mór) means 'big'. Bigshitville is now our Hampstead.

At the lower end of the road lived the workers who sustained the shipyard and built the *Titanic*. When men came back from the battlefields of France and Belgium after the Great War catholics were chased out of their jobs to make room for loyal protestants who had fought for the empire.

That catholics had fought in the war too, while other Irish catholics had been fighting for independence in the south, was easily overlooked. Catholics and protestants had fought side by side in the trenches and come home to an Ireland whose traditional divisions had reasserted themselves. Their fellow feeling and comradeship with protestant soldiers was now an embarrassment.

If we walk through the town, I can show you the grandiose City Hall and the stone buildings of the presbyterian assembly, some of the old linen mills and the great sandstone central library, and you can see that this city was once a wealthy mercantile centre with riches to spare for ornamentation and culture.

Or we can go down some of the alleyways to find an old pub where we can sit among office workers and shoppers to enjoy a bowl of chowder and a glass of stout. The drinkers and diners will not know by looking at us whether we are protestant or catholic, nor will most care, though if we discuss sectarianism or politics we will speak softly so as not to be overheard. No one will be invasively curious or unfriendly. This is neutral territory – but it is better than that. It is friendly. All around us the main roads and the housing estates right out to the edge of the city and beyond define themselves as catholic or protestant, nationalist or unionist, and yet there is not a trace of the demarcating instinct in the city centre.

Though, if a couple of young men walked into the pub in football jerseys we'd all look up, anxious. Gruff, potentially violent sectarianism is working class. The middle classes may harbour their prejudices so close they are hardly aware of them.

No one comes into a pub for lunch in the hopes of having a fight as well. No one asks an attendant in Marks & Spencer for directions to the changing room and wonders at the same time if she or he is a catholic or a protestant. Well, some do, maybe.

We have our native little ways of telling who's what, from accent to manners and humour or clothes, but they are hardly efficient.

This is the hardest part to explain to an outsider. Belfast is a sectarian city. We may assume that many of these people when they go home are content to live in a sectarian milieu on their segregated estates but clearly they are comfortable outside it too.

Most fear no one. That is not what we mean by a sectarian city. Most sectarianism is collective, not individual. You meet few real bigots. Yet the threat from the few means that whole communities have to be walled off against each other.

Some divided communities in other countries suffer the complication of physical distinction between the people of the factions. Belfast would be easier to read if protestants and catholics had different skin colour. Then it might not be possible to have the relaxed mingling in the city centre and they might divide into separate bars. Or if they had different attire, the way in which you can distinguish a hindu from a muslim in Uttar Pradesh, we would be perpetually aware of difference. But there are no strong distinguishing features to warn you in Belfast that you are not among your own, not until you start talking to each other.

Some may adopt football shirts or tattoos to advertise their tribal allegiance. In most city centre bars the young man in a football top will not be served. The tattoo will be discreetly covered.

Now let's go up the Falls.

Belfast is like a wheel with spokes, with main roads running from the centre in all directions out to the suburbs. The Falls starts at Castle Street, which is a continuation of High Street which is built on the old river.

From the bottom of Castle Street we can travel all the way out to Twinbrook and beyond without ever having to take a turn. All of that area is catholic.

That is not to say that everyone there would identify as a catholic believer or be happy with the word 'catholic' as an ethnic label, but there are very few who have not been baptised in a catholic church, who have not attended or do not send their children to catholic schools, who will not be buried according to the rites of the Catholic Church.

Immediately we step into Castle Street I feel that we have crossed into a ghetto. Nearly all of the people here heading home are catholics going deeper into a catholic area. This is also a rough and shabby shopping area for some who aren't going on into the more diffuse and indefinable space of the mixed city. Here are shops enough for them. Here also are a few pubs and there is an air of dereliction. In the evening there are the alcoholics and the drug users. You don't go far without someone asking if you have any change and you keep walking because the decrepitude of the desperate looks dangerous.

I am displaying prejudice here, disdaining the poor and the bored who perhaps have come here to find each other, some perhaps looking for reckless, perhaps criminal distraction.

Catholic west Belfast is not uniform in any way. There are estates of public housing and enclaves of home ownership. All classes are there, apart, perhaps, from the very rich. There is no way to sum up the area. The only generalisation you can make is that nearly all people there are baptised catholics and most of those among them who vote, vote for Sinn Féin, the political party whose modern form grew out of the IRA.

There are a few nice shops in Castle Street; the delicatessen, the more elegant lounge bar. They remind you that this was once a more salubrious part of town, the beginning of the centre rather than what it feels like now, the end of the ghetto.

Probably all of the people at the bus stop are catholics. Some are migrants from Poland and Lithuania whose Catholicism has no local political relevance. And there are a few of Asian and African backgrounds, but so far only a few.

All of the people at the taxi rank are going to catholic areas. This is a fixed route, a fixed-fare taxi service. Black cabs which in other parts of town would be wandering freely across different areas were established here as an alternative to the bus service when the buses were taken off because of rioting.

Soon we pass the ring road and are into Divis Street where it fades into the Falls Road. There is the tower block and the double-spired cathedral. And across the road the old hostel for homeless drunks.

This area was a battlefield. I can tell you how I stood here during one of the riots at the start of the Troubles and watched men throw petrol bombs from the top of the tower block. I can show you the bullet strikes in the old redbrick primary school.

Look up each of the side streets and you will see gates barring the way through to the road that runs parallel with the Falls, the Shankill, where the protestants live. No one is stopping you going there, of course, but each point of access between the two roads can be closed to secure each from the other.

This area around us now is the lower Falls, mostly residential to our left as we head out of town, shopping centres and industrial units on the right. It is not a lovely area, though we can see Black Mountain and Divis from here. There is history and propaganda in the wall murals that associate the local armed factions with international causes, treating the demand for Irish reunification as on a spiritual par with resistance to apartheid in South Africa or the cause of the Palestinians.

Tourists come to see this wall and be photographed in front of it, associating themselves with an IRA hero they'd probably not heard of until the tour guide pointed him out.

Here on the left is the memorial garden in honour of D Company of the Provisional IRA with a black wall bearing the names of those who got killed or accidentally blew themselves up during the Troubles and the dates on which they died. Anniversaries here are marked with flag-lowering ceremonies by slack-bodied, sentimental old republicans in black berets. They say the rosary for their fallen comrades.

At the crossroads there is the big hospital on one side and the convent school on the other. The hospital, right in the heart of a catholic area, is for everybody and protestants will cross town to avail of it, as catholics will sometimes cross the Shankill to reach the catholic hospital, the Mater. Medicine is neutral.

The convent is almost vacant now. No young woman wants to be a nun these days. The girls in their burgundy uniforms will do A levels and go to university. They will be teachers and doctors and solicitors. Almost all of those girls were baptised catholic. What they actually believe is for them to say. The university most will go to is Queen's University in Belfast where the students are catholic, though no one consciously determined that that should be so.

It's different at the teacher training college next door to the school. It is a catholic college for providing catholic teachers for catholic children in catholic schools.

There is another teacher training college as part of the university. It was set up to provide non-denominational education, mostly in state schools, which are mostly protestant schools. Between these two colleges we train too many teachers and can't provide jobs for all of them.

We could go further out along the road and I could show you the cemeteries and some of the historically interesting graves like those of IRA members. I could show you the murals commemorating the IRA and the memorials to the dead. Much of west Belfast is like a theme park to militant republicanism.

But let's turn here and go up the Springfield and across to the protestant Shankill.

We can pass through the peace line without difficulty. It isn't closed most of the time, though the big metal gates form an impregnable barrier when it is shut and bolted. The area on both sides of the gate is waste ground, but carry on through, past the bleak space, and you come to a T-junction off a busy road.

Nowhere in the real world would you just stumble out of bleak dereliction into a thriving commercial centre like this. Property this close to shops and offices and dense population should logically be valuable and in demand.

We are going to turn down the Shankill and back towards the centre of town.

There is a good view of the mountain now behind us, more like two rounded peaks huddled together. Just to our right is the ornate old library and across from that the community centre.

Just as the Falls Road has its memorial murals commemorating paramilitary gangs, there are gable walls here adorned with portraits of men with guns, rolls of honour listing the dead of different groups described as companies, battalions and brigades. There is symmetry here between communities which insist that they are different from each other. A memorial garden contains tributes to those killed by IRA bombs in pubs on this road, in a fishmonger's and in a furniture store.

No one on either side of the peace line is allowed to forget history, at least the history of inter-communal murder. You pass it as you go out shopping or walking to school.

The flags here are the Union flag and the Ulster flag, a red hand at the centre of a red cross on a white background, which is not the same as the flag of the province of Ulster, which has a yellow background and represents the whole province of Ulster, three of whose counties are in the Irish Republic.

And there are the routine reminders that people have other concerns, the other fishmonger's that supplies fancy restaurants and smokes its own salmon, the leisure centre, the vegetable shop with its stalls out on the footpath. There are fast food shops and pharmacies. Not so many bookshops.

I can point out to you the pubs that are favoured by loyalist paramilitaries. If you don't mind, we'll not go in.

Nearly all the people here are protestant, which is not to say that they are believing christians. There are more diverse churches on the Shankill than on the Falls, for Protestantism includes various congregations, from the Presbyterian to the Methodist and the Church of Ireland and the smaller evangelical Churches, the Elim Pentecostal, the Baptist, the Free Presbyterian and more. That homogeneity of Catholicism worries the protestants because it suggests to them that catholics are a more coherent community, a church-bound obedient people. And while they were a minority in Northern Ireland compared to protestants, they were a solidly united people, in the protestant imagination, in a way that protestants themselves never could be.

It was often claimed through the Troubles period that the driving force behind IRA violence was the Catholic Church. This was an idea that catholics themselves found bizarre, when voiced by orangemen or the ranting preacher Ian Paisley, yet they were perhaps not taking into account how Catholic Church rules requiring children of mixed marriages to be raised catholic had the effect of eroding a protestant community.

As in Castle Street, where we moved from the city centre into the lower Falls area and passed through a depleted and cheap-looking area, we pass now into a similar space as we leave the Shankill and go back into town.

Communities have been separated by open space and sometimes by the otherwise unnecessary widening of roads where walls would not have done the job. You can see this in other areas too, like at Short Strand, where protestant and catholic people are kept at a distance from each other by town planners having turned a small road into a multi-lane highway for just a few hundred yards to expand the space between catholic and protestant housing.

This is a city shaped to accommodate division.

*

I have just shown you a small part of it. I could take you to Derry where the catholics live mostly on one side of the river and protestants on the other. I could take you to a country hillside and have a farmer show you how he reads the landscape as divided into Orange and Green fields, farms that belong to protestants, farms that belong to catholics. I could take you to holiday resorts favoured by catholics and others favoured by protestants, where people feel they can drink and chatter at night among their own.

And you may say that this is normal, that cities all over the world have their Chinatowns and Little Italys. There are English places like the suburb of Savile Town in Dewsbury in West Yorkshire which is wholly Asian while Chickenley a mile down the road is white because it is the instinct of the migrant to seek out the familiar. But this is different. These Northern Irish communities are indigenous, going back centuries. The Chinatowns of the USA emerged in the mid-nineteenth century and are dissolving now. The biggest of them, in New York, has a population of around half a million, about a fifteenth of the whole city population.

Belfast's protestant and catholic communities cover almost the whole of the city between them.

Migrant communities have formed here too, with jews settling mostly around the Antrim Road and Chinese people settling together in Donegall Pass. And the catholic communities in Belfast formed in much the same way, but these were migrants from the country areas or from the south and west of Ireland who moved to the city in the nineteenth and twentieth centuries. They were Irish people who came from other divided communities in other parts of Ireland.

Periodic sectarian violence drove stragglers back into their ghettos so it was the least sectarian, the ones who didn't mind living with the other side, who suffered most. I saw that upheaval in my own lifetime, in the sixties and seventies when catholics who lived in predominantly protestant areas were driven from their homes or fled out of caution when fires burned nearby.

I saw my protestant neighbours move out. I saw the lorry stacked with furniture while a man in a balaclava mask watched from the other side of the street and neighbours hugged as they said goodbye. The threat was not from the people closest to them but from organised militias.

Sectarian violence is a complex phenomenon. We have nothing against you personally, they will say; we'll even help you to move. No one likes to be called sectarian or to admit to sectarian hatred, but they will say they understand the forces that divide society, and even though they have friends on the other side, they will understand why one community has to be shored up against another.

They will say, the peace lines have not been erected to protect you against me. I wish you no harm at all but I'll not let you take down that wall. It's not that we are bigots but we are not ready.

East Belfast established itself as protestant around the heavy industries of ship building and the rope works. Or was it that the areas were protestant first and the industries took their character by recruiting locally? Whatever, a catholic had little to no expectation of getting a job there.

West Belfast expanded through migration from the South and the country areas. My father was a barman and my mother was a nurse. My brothers and sisters took jobs in the civil service. One out of the six of us went into industry while I became a journalist and another a social worker. That was probably the typical catholic family experience, taking work that required a bit of education. My generation was the first to get that education for free.

The protestants of the east were more deeply rooted in Belfast and perhaps saw us as encroaching on their territory. They worried about catholics having larger families and anticipated us outbreeding them then voting them into a united Ireland.

2

Sectarianism

I became aware of sectarianism at about the age of ten or eleven. I was playing with other children from our estate, Riverdale, on the embankment of the railway track at Finaghy Halt, just south-west of Belfast city centre. We used to roll down the grassy slopes and dare each other to get closer to the thick iron tracks. Bigger boys would dare us to put an ear to the metal rim to pick up the hum of an oncoming train. We thought of that space as fascinatingly dangerous but with the danger being one that we could back away from, screaming with mock terror, any time we chose.

There was another danger there which we were only aware of through the talk of other boys, that we hadn't known directly and didn't quite believe in: protestants. The protestants we knew in Riverdale were nice people.

Mind you, we did know they were protestants and different.

One day near the railway line there was a little boy who probably was a bit younger than me. He had black hair and a woolly jumper and short trousers and he looked unhappy. He was playing on his own with a knife, flinging it into the ground, practising. That in itself was not alarming. We all had penknives then, even daggers that we wore at our sides on our belts and played games with them or whittled sticks, imagining ourselves to be the Lone Ranger or Tonto taking some control of the wildness.

We were curious about the boy and approached him. Maybe he'd let us see his knife.

He said, 'Are youse fenians?'

This puzzled me. I had been reading about the fenians. I knew the word. They were a nineteenth-century rebel movement. No, we weren't fenians. I was the show-off who told him that and thereby answered the question for him. I had confirmed we were 'fenians' by knowing our rebel history. I suppose the word may have come back into usage at their centenary in 1957.

'Youse are fuckin' fenians.' And he stabbed into the air in front of him. 'Fuck off back to where youse came from.'

That was the most serious confrontation I had known until then. When we fought among ourselves we wrestled and rolled on the ground and twisted arms and said, 'Do you submit?' And when one submitted we both got up again and bragged about how well we had done or nearly done.

It's easy to imagine now that the boy was in a sore mood before he had seen us. We know better now that some children live miserable lives. And maybe if he thought we fenians might come in the night to kill him, he was afraid. Maybe that's how his mother told him to go to sleep. 'Be quiet or fenians will come and get you.' In our house it was the bogeyman you had to be wary of attracting. We were having fun, not out to fight with anyone. Perhaps someone had told him that fenians would stab you in the back; that they're not to be trusted. They hate us.

So now we understood that we had crossed the divide, not just the divide from a catholic area to a protestant one but the divide between innocence of sectarianism and knowledge of it, the sort of knowledge that removes you from the garden. My mother always warned us to be careful when going to Finaghy but I assumed that was because of the trains. She had never sat down with me and explained that there were protestants who might not like us playing in their area, near their homes.

We had been advised to be careful how we spoke to our protestant neighbours and not to be asking them rude questions about their religion or threatening them with a united Ireland. People had to get on with each other. That was the way. You have to apply a degree of civility in dealings with protestants to assure them you are no threat to them and to prevent any arguments arising. So you don't talk about religion and politics. You don't argue about whether Derry is Derry or Londonderry.

Once you know about sectarianism you are part of it. As a young catholic you look out for protestants, assess how you might offend or put yourself at risk. Not all protestants, of course; everybody knows that. But from now on you'll take your time about getting to know them, just in case.

But on that day one of us was big enough to step forward and say, 'Fuck off, you wee proddy bastard, or I'll shove that knife down your throat,' and he turned and ran away. It was not an end to the drama that was going to teach me anything.

Sometimes sectarianism is civil. The exaggerated conscious-ness of difference inclines people towards consideration, a determination not to annoy the other, even to put the other at ease, sometimes by dropping hints to alert the other to the difference in case something might be said that would make it too explicit.

'You be nice to each other,' my mother said. 'And sometimes you stay out of their way. Let them get on with whatever they're doing. Like the Twelfth.'

Every year the Orange Order's Twelfth of July parade came almost up to our estate, up the Finaghy Road, over the railway bridge and down our side of it and turned into a field that the M1 now slices through. It was a massive parade that would take three hours at least to pass you standing on the road if you were brave enough to stand near it, for we feared they could curse you with a look.

Actually the Twelfth excited me. I could not help but be intensely curious about these people who were alien to us, doing something huge that we could be no part of, that we wanted no part of. It was our way to be contemptuous of them as it was theirs to be wary of us. But I went to the field and I picked up empty glass lemonade bottles and took them back to the shops to get money on them and I sometimes talked to the orangemen and even argued history with them and they indulged me.

'Why are you talking to them about the Easter Rising for God's sake? Do you want strung up? Just stay away from them. For your own sake.'

But it is normal for a man to be bemused by a boy who takes an interest, even a coarsely informed, hostile interest, in what he is doing.

So one explained the image on his banner, William crossing the Boyne.

'To kill catholics!'

'Will you promise me you'll read your history?' said the man. 'It's not simple. And people have not come here because they are bad people. And we don't think you and yours are bad people either.'

All the children sitting at the desks around me in school were catholics. There was a crucifix on one wall and a statue of the Virgin Mary on another. Every school day began and ended with prayers. When the new school opened, the huge assembly hall was used for masses that the chapel was not big enough to accommodate as new housing estates went up around us for more and more catholics.

That school had been built with the help of a school building fund that our families paid into so that catholics could have a system separate from the state's.

Keeping detached from the state wasn't always easy. A new library was built at the top of Slieveban Drive. We were so eager to get into it that we resembled a mob to the staff within and they locked the doors. What little savages they must have thought we were!

The next day we were processed to a special mass and a lecture from the furious parish priest bellowing 'Shame on you' from the pulpit. We had let ourselves down in front of the protestants who staffed the library. We had disgraced the school and the parish. This was serious beyond our comprehension.

It would now be an extension of our teacher's responsibility to police our visits to the library and approve the books we were taking out before we could present them to the nice woman at the desk to be stamped. That system didn't last long and the library turned out to be no great threat to the formation of our catholic moral consciences nor we to it.

The point of this intervention was essentially the same as my mother's advice on how to deal with protestants. We had always to behave properly in front of them, not to let contention arise, not to let ourselves down, for in doing so we were not just disgracing ourselves but reinforcing the prejudices we presumed them to have that we were a thick and ignorant rabble peasantry bent on violence against them.

Today some parents try to raise their children in ignorance of sectarianism. They time their holidays to avoid the festivities. I know people who grew up into their twenties in Belfast without ever seeing the parades.

Sectarianism is not always bitter and hateful but it is always an excessive consciousness of difference in another person.

We joke about sectarianism. That humour has now been shared with English audiences through comedy in the TV series *Derry Girls*. The girls on their way to a church-led reconciliation project at which they will meet protestants express their nerves and their curiosity. Protestants are people they have heard talked about darkly or in hushed tones. My father, a Derry man, would speak of 'your own' and 'the other sort'. The girls wonder if there will be enough protestants to go round them all. They whisper about sectarianism the way they do about sex. They giggle about what they fear and don't quite understand but which they know they will have to deal with.

There are times when the consciousness of difference is not controlled and the joke doesn't work.

I was standing in a queue in the BBC canteen in Belfast. This was in the nineties. A producer in front of me with his tray was waiting for the serving woman to fetch something, maybe something that was being reheated or another tray of salmon steaks. Whatever. I moved round him to the coffee machine, effectively jumping the queue, and he turned and said, 'You fenians now think you own the place.' And he laughed to assure me that he was joking.

But why would he joke about a difference between us if the difference did not play on his mind?

He would never have said, you blue-eyed people think you own the place, or you woolly jumper types, you bearded people now think you own the place. That would have been neither funny nor offensive, but simply ridiculous.

You fenians thinking you own the place – that puts you in a distinct category that everyone is familiar with and most people politely resolve not to mention. Every good joke is transgressive so this might have been carried off as a successful undermining of our hypocritical civilities. But I thought that in the BBC we had outgrown those civilities, so what was left to joke about? Either I was wrong, and the civilities were still in place, the mannered negotiation of every situation to avoid offence, and that meant that people around me were indeed over-conscious of my being a catholic. Or this one man had got it wrong and carried an over-anxious awareness of me being a catholic and couldn't contain it. He had tried to make a joke of it and it hadn't worked. So he was a bigot, though maybe a bigot struggling his way out of bigotry much as teenagers make gross jokes about sex and fail to impress.

I could have made a complaint and perhaps had him

sacked. I could have walked out of the building myself and declared that it was a hostile working environment and I could have claimed compensation. I would have got money, perhaps quite a lot, more than a year's earnings anyway to cushion me until I found work in an organisation which was more genial.

I did not complain about the sectarian jibe from the BBC producer because my own experience in the BBC had educated me in how to recognise my own sectarian thinking. One of my closest colleagues was a presbyterian minister called Bert. When I came out with some remark about the outrageous bigotry of unionist politicians or an evangelical protestant who thought the pope was the anti-Christ, Bert would quietly say, 'Well, look at it from his perspective...'

He reminded me that people who are neighbourly and civil may have vastly contrasting world views, that the kindly clergyman who has poked his head round the door to say hello before going into a meeting with the Head of Department lives with a settled understanding that you – and the Head of Department, being a catholic – are going to burn in Hell for all eternity. Interaction with people who thought like that was part of my routine work and I never once met one who gloated over my misfortune.

Having got so much from the BBC to broaden my own consciousness, I was not going to retaliate against someone else whose best chance of learning to understand others was probably in that same institution.

Friends have joked about me being an 'uppity taig' and I have laughed with them. 'Taig' is a derogatory word for an Irish catholic, usually used by protestants. A joke like that might work, might even signal that the friend is completely relaxed among taigs, if it is not laboured. But discriminatory sexist or racist language is often passed off as banter and those who take offence are then accused of lacking a sense of humour.

In working-class Belfast banter was always intended to challenge. It was usually about pulling someone into line with the cultural consensus. A young person may feel glad of banter, appreciate it as the chiding way in which he or she was inducted into the cultural norms and alerted to the danger of looking foolish or eccentric.

In a place like Belfast where banter is intrinsic to our humour, that it is always wrong is a hard lesson to learn. It used to be that being 'able to take a joke' was the mark of a decent person who could fit in with the group. Perhaps it still is.

There is some humour which enters into sectarianism, and humour which mocks it.

Any teasing of a friend in the mildest way for being a bit of a taig or a prod (protestant) takes excessive note of the otherness of the person addressed and is sectarian. But if the distance between people is real they shouldn't ignore it. Some admit to being sectarian but seek to minimise it or laugh at it. It never feels safe to admit to being sectarian and to work through it. The poet John Hewitt, an older contemporary of Seamus Heaney and Derek Mahon, wrote several poems airing his uneasiness among the catholic Irish. Was he a bigot confessing to being a bigot or a decent man wrestling with a difficulty he wished to resolve?

And can someone be blamed for trying to work through sectarian feeling and not being able to lightly shrug off all their conditioning? Many of my generation in Ireland would have been in their thirties or forties before ever having a conversation with a black person or someone from Asia. They didn't enter into those conversations oblivious of colour and culture. They stared. They had questions in their minds that they were afraid to ask. If you are black, how can you tell that your hands are clean? People think these things.

I recognise unfamiliarity as the problem when someone overtly notices that I am of a catholic background, even if they are commenting on it while attempting to make me feel welcome, as has happened when I have given talks to church or community groups in protestant areas. If someone is at ease with me being a catholic, why would they mention it at all? And it still happens, which suggests that there are people who even in adult life have little familiarity with the other side.

If they are not at ease, is that their fault, given that they may have been raised in suspicion?

Then there is the joke which undermines sectarianism. An example is that episode of *Derry Girls* where the protestant and catholic schoolchildren are brought together to help them get to know each other. They are asked to name characteristics that they perceive in each other's communities and their answers are written on a blackboard. The children make anodyne and silly observations. Catholics eat fish on Friday. Protestants like soup. Protestants keep the toaster in a cupboard and say a bit extra at the end of the Our Father. Catholics love statues. These answers are safe, however. None is so blatant and angry that passions would be roused by it.

They might have said, catholics think they can commit any sin, even murder, and that a priest can put them right with God again. Which they do. Or catholics think you're a hero if you have been in jail. Or protestants think they are going to go to Heaven and all the catholics are going to Hell. Remarks like these would have been too close to representing actual familiar prejudices to work in a comedy sketch.

Northern Ireland loved that *Derry Girls* blackboard joke and a replica of the board was exhibited in the Ulster Museum in 2019. That must mean something. I think the joke was popular because it absolves us of our sectarianism. It presents prejudice as ludicrous rather than hostile or toxic, and we like that because it confronts nothing in us that we would feel we had actually to defend. It is a safe parody. Keep your toaster in your cupboard if you like. Who cares? An equivalent might be a racist character in a play whose racism is so ridiculous that even real, bitter racists could laugh at it and feel assured that they are not as bad as they might be. Another example of this absolving humour is a tape made by loyalists in Belfast, a song called 'The Pope's a Darkie'. Of course, no one actually believes that the pope is black. The joke represents protestant sectarianism and racism as ridiculous yet the song was written to be performed to loyalist protestant audiences, not to offend catholics.

In one sense it says, you accuse me of bigotry, well, get a load of this. The accused, instead of apologising or giving any credibility to the accusation, goes the other way and amplifies the bigotry into the appalling, beyond what anyone actually believes. The joke challenges the liberal who pontificates about how awful sectarianism is. At the same time, it so misrepresents actual sectarianism that no protestant in the audience is embarrassed by it, their authentic bigotry untouched.

The joke would almost have worked better if it was delivered by catholics as a parody of protestant sectarianism.

Contrast that humour with another joke that came out of loyalist culture: What's the difference between a taig and an onion? Answer: You don't cry when you slice a taig. That's humour that is totally unapologetic about sectarianism. You'll only laugh at that in safe company among like-minded friends.

Sectarianism is reinforced by songs. Both republican and orange traditions are deeply imbued with propagandist music.

In the early Troubles, the various republican factions – and the Provisional IRA was only one of several then – organised shebeens and drinking clubs in the areas from which they operated. They had music sessions in the bars where they gathered, from the Old

House in Albert Street to the Green Briar up the Glen Road. And the songs they sang were 'The Broad Black Brimmer', 'Johnson's Motor Car', 'Rifles of the IRA' and more.

The core message of all these songs was that the IRA was a noble and decent, good-humoured bunch of fellas with a long tradition that warrants respect. When we drank in those pubs and clubs we were being invited to join in the nostalgia for the freedom struggle and to endorse its continuation.

'It's just a broad black brimmer, its ribbons frayed and torn'.

This song imagines a young man's mother proudly dressing him in the IRA uniform of his dead father.

It would be hard to measure the impact of those songs on the republican consciousness but it was probably very great indeed.

A few jars down you and you're on your feet singing along to 'Kevin Barry', or 'Boolavogue', and you're ready to saunter home with your heart welling with pride in the old unchanging Irish struggle. And in Orangeism, song plays the same role of connecting the present to the past and persuading followers that they are part of an ancient struggle.

'It was worn at Derry, Aughrim, Enniskillen and the Boyne.'

These musical traditions are history lessons, and if the history isn't exactly as the books tell it, who cares?

'But we loosed our guns upon them, and quickly won the day / So we knocked five hundred Papishes right over Dolly's Brae.'

That's how we'll remember it. And 'we'll wade knee deep in fenian blood' and there'll be no surrender.

The songs bind people together within their sectarian culture and commit them to maintaining it. They dismiss any squeamishness about violence and they assert that the war goes on today as it has for hundreds of years.

'I met with Napper Tandy / and he took me by the hand.'

You can walk with your hand in Napper Tandy's from the eighteenth century to the twenty-first and perhaps the twenty-second too.

There are parodies of sectarianism in drama and satire but they often seem to encourage the audience into a smug comfort that they are not quite as bad as the targets of the joke. Sectarianism is good rich material for satire, but satire can never represent it as the worst that it can be.

For instance, I once saw a woman berate children for playing with a catholic. 'Why are you playing with a taig? You know he is a taig.' This was during the worst of the Troubles so people were angry and afraid. I can't believe this would happen today.

And a little boy pleads, 'No, missus, I didn't know he was a taig.'

How do you make a joke out of that?

As a reporter I covered the long-running picket on a catholic church in Harryville in Ballymena. I asked a group of protesters why they were protesting against a church and a boy shrieked at me, 'It's not a church. It's a fenian hole.'

Sectarianism can only be funny when it is parodied and diminished. And doing that colludes in the pretence that it is really not very serious, merely the preoccupation of stupid people.

Perhaps that was the real problem with the character Alf Garnett, the absurd racist in the BBC sitcom *Till Death Us Do Part* broadcast between 1965 and 1975. By parodying racism, depicting it as merely ridiculous, he was undermining efforts to speak seriously about it.

I have joked with protestant friends that they are too literal minded, that they have attitudes which are characteristic of their protestant background. Sometimes they will agree with a criticism like that, accepting that the difference of which we are overly conscious is real. Social attitude surveys show up more legalistic thinking among protestants, more liberal attitudes among catholics. The theology of protestants is more biblically based; that of catholics more founded on church teachings and later revelations like apparitions of the Virgin Mary. These are the things my mother warned me not to talk to them about.

Also many catholics today will say that the IRA was justified, or at least excusable, in its terrorist campaign. The Sinn Féin deputy leader Michelle O'Neill has said there was no alternative to the IRA campaign. Protestants are much less likely to be as indulgent of the terrorism of their neighbours in the loyalist paramilitaries, though more likely to defend the police and army against the charge that they were unreasonably and criminally violent which, occasionally, they were.

Trevor Ringland, a solicitor and former Ireland rugby international, says, 'How do I cope with the fact that if someone had put a bomb under my father's car because he was a policeman and killed me along with him, many of my catholic friends would make excuses for that, even revere the memory of the bomber if the blast had taken him too?'

He is entitled to that unease, although among his catholic friends it would be, as my mother advised, better to avoid the subject.

When I went to work among protestants during the Troubles I was aware that some who were otherwise friendly and helpful were sharing little about their private lives with me. That might have been because they had a police officer or a soldier in the family. It was better for them to keep a distance from someone who went home to a housing estate controlled by the IRA than to risk that information which might help to target a policeman might get passed on through him, even inadvertently.

Should I have been insulted?

Later I met a police officer who had befriended a Donegal man on holiday and travelled frequently to meet him and share a sporting interest. The officer told me that he had never revealed to his friend what his job was. Wouldn't the friend have a right to be insulted if he found out? He might rightly suspect that he was put at risk of exposing secrets to the Royal Ulster Constabulary (RUC), was perhaps even being manipulated as an intelligence asset.

The point about this civil and mannered sectarianism is that it is about containing relationships which might overheat, for there is huge hurt in both communities as a consequence of awful sectarian violence.

3

The Hate

At the end of May 2022, the Orange Order organised a parade to mark the centenary of Northern Ireland. This was inevitably a sectarianised concern. Nationalists had made clear their determination to make no contribution to the celebration of the formation of the state.

I went down to Queen's Bridge to watch the parade pass by, orangemen in their regalia, marching bands of young men.

A few days later someone posted on Twitter a video of people who had taken part in the parade, in a hall bedecked with banners, drinking cans of beer and singing. The song they sang was a mockery of a young woman called Michaela McAreavey and her husband.

On their honeymoon, eleven years before this, the couple had gone to Mauritius. There Michaela was murdered in their hotel room. Someone wrote this lurid song mocking the tragedy.

She went to her room to get a wee treat,

a bunch of strangers she did meet.

They hammered and they hammered and they beat

  her about,

John McAreavey didn't hear her shout.

The man who led the singing in the hall stood up and rallied others around him to join in. Some presented raised fist salutes, like the Nazi sign but with the fist clenched. Some looked bewildered and disengaged. But many seemed to know the words. Some laughed when they reached the punchline. One balding man with his glasses pushed back onto his head laughed at the last line and clapped his hands then rubbed his face with both hands as if in some kind of elated state of shock. Then he caught the eye of a friend at a neighbouring table and they laughed together, as if with permission from each other. They knew that this was outrageous and it was probably beyond what they were used to but they were loving the dark mischief of it. Three others at the same table laughed and clapped.

The hall was crowded with people of all ages. It is clear in the video that about half the people in view are not taking part. A woman sitting opposite the man standing and leading the singing takes no part in it. Others at his table look around embarrassed, giving their companion no support.

There was a mystery here.

Why would anyone have sat down to write such a song, to mock a young woman who was murdered on her honeymoon, to effectively endorse her killing, indeed to celebrate it? Were these not men with sisters and daughters, wives or girlfriends? How could they laugh at the thought of a woman being 'hammered'?

They did not know Michaela McAreavey or have any personal reason to despise her. She was not a public figure so most people had not heard of her until her murder was reported. They would, however, have known about her father, Mickey Harte. He was the manager of a successful Tyrone GAA team that has won the All-Ireland football final four times.

The GAA, or Gaelic Athletic Association, promotes Gaelic sport and culture. It is almost wholly catholic, though it has been more accommodating of difference in recent years. It has named sports grounds after republican revolutionaries. I grew up near Casement Park, named after Sir Roger Casement, a British diplomat who was hanged as a traitor for trying to import guns from Germany for the Irish Volunteers in 1916, when Britain was at war with Germany.

Occasionally sectarian attitudes break through in the GAA too. After the 2022 All-Ireland hurling final celebrating supporters sang IRA songs which were also videoed and posted to Twitter.

After the murder of Michaela McAreavey, the DUP leader and the first minister of Northern Ireland Peter Robinson, accompanied by his successor Arlene Foster, had visited the home of Michaela's grieving family to offer condolences. That was seen in Northern Ireland as a significant gesture. Actually in a healthy society not riven like this, the visit to the Harte home to commiserate with them in the loss of a daughter would not be a major news story; would not have deep meaning read into it; would not be a sign of a change occurring in the character of the region.

Were the men singing the ghastly song airing their contempt for Harte and for Gaelic culture and sport?

Were they sneering at softer unionists having joined in the mourning?

Were they responding to a sense that 'the other side' had gained some moral credit from the celebration of the life of a beautiful young woman from the Gaelic heartland, and scoffing at it?

Was misogyny as much a part of their contempt for her as sectarianism?

Loyalism has been savage with women and some of the most gruesome of loyalist murders have been of women.

Anne Marie Smyth, a twenty-six-year-old catholic, went to a football supporters' club, apparently oblivious to the danger. This was in 1992, two years before the first ceasefire of the peace process. She was brought afterwards to a house party by UVF men where they strangled her and cut her throat. They dumped her body on waste ground.

Margaret Wright was a protestant murdered in a loyalist band hall in 1994. She was thirty-three years old. The people in the hall wrongly assumed that she was a catholic. She was beaten and tortured in the hall in front of the drinkers, with women taking part. They stripped her of her clothes, apart from her knickers apparently, shot her in the head and dumped her body in a wheelie bin.

These are now historic events but one can hardly be confident that a catholic woman would have been safe among the men celebrating the murder of Michaela McAreavey.

I messaged a liberal unionist and asked if he could explain the singing of the song. He said, 'It's appalling, I would say that there are about 2–3 singing and a few cheering on but most are probably unaware of the words. Alcohol and hate, one antagoniser, and then a few weak men join in. They're scum for doing this, it won't represent any Orangeman that I know but that will fall on deaf ears.'

He gave me a quote from the rules of the Orange Order that said members should be 'ever abstaining from all uncharitable words, actions or sentiments towards all Roman Catholics'.

I think he underestimated the enthusiasm for the song in the hall, though maybe a few were just carried along by the energy and were not fully aware of what they were cheering. But he was right to think that orangemen generally would be held accountable for this. That was clear from many of the tweets in response to it.

Wallace Thompson is a member of the Independent Orange Order and marched in the centenary parade that day. He is a conservative christian, the type that regards homosexuality and abortion as sinful. He was one of the founder members, in his youth, of the Democratic Unionist Party and a close associate of Rev. Ian Paisley. He was later an advisor to the senior DUP member Nigel Dodds when he was minister of social development in the Northern Ireland Assembly executive. He also founded the Caleb Foundation to represent small evangelical churches in their claims for more media coverage.

He says of the parade, 'Most of it was absolutely fine – very dignified and family friendly. But there were certain times to be honest, I was cringing because the bands were playing the 'Billy Boys' and the crowds were singing the words, and I was thinking, this is awful, awful.'

The 'Billy Boys' song rallies loyalists to 'wade knee deep in fenian blood'.

Orange bands will often play songs which have familiar inoffensive tunes but which are sung with nasty sectarian lyrics. The song about Michaela McAreavey was to the tune of a familiar Belfast street song about Mickey Marley's Roundabout. Marley toured the streets with a horse-drawn carousel that children could pay to take a ride on.

Wallace says, 'There were young people with bottles or glasses of drink in their hands but there it is. Then you see that video coming out at Dundonald Orange Hall and you think, there's a problem here. There's a hatred here. I am associated with that broader community and yet I can't – not only can I not condone it; I just have to robustly oppose it.'

He says he knows that there are nasty songs 'on the other side too'. 'But that's not my responsibility. I have to call it for what it is. True evangelical Protestantism cannot condone that sort of sectarianism. Doctrinal difference? Yes. Criticism of roman catholic worship? Yes, in a certain context. But those boys singing the song wouldn't have the first clue. That's a sad thing about it.'

This is interesting. He doesn't identity with the harsh sectarianism of those who sang the song, would never dream of singing such a song himself, and yet he feels a responsibility to condemn it that is different from what he would feel if the singers had been catholics mocking the murder of a protestant woman. Obviously he would be appalled by such a thing but would feel included among those targeted rather than potentially implicated in the abuse itself. What he is saying is that those louts are, to some degree, his people and he must condemn them or be included in the criticism of them.

Wallace also speaks of secular sectarianism as something distinct from the celebration of Protestantism that, he believes, the Orange institution is for. Orangeism has gone astray and lost sight of its primary concern, which should be religion, the promotion and celebration of the protestant faith. No good protestant would scoff at the murder of anyone.

Actually, many nationalists saw the song as a revelation of what Orangeism is really about.

The walls of the hall where the song was sung were decked with orange banners, and the video shows one of them clearly. It is a portrait of Late Bro. Walter McFarland on a purple banner with the heading 'Dundonald Purple Vine LOL [Loyal Orange Lodge] 1056'.

Now nationalists could say, this is what they are all like. We see that same criticism on social media every time there is evidence of protestant sectarianism, and there is a lot of it every July when loyalists build huge bonfires for Eleventh Night and frequently burn the Irish tricolour and election posters of nationalist and republican politicians.

Máiría Cahill, a writer from a republican family who criticises that tradition, challenged the 'all the same' argument. Attributing sectarian nastiness to everyone who marches on the Twelfth, she said, was the equivalent of loyalists treating all catholics at the West Belfast Festival as supporters of the IRA.

On the morning after the video appeared the BBC reported that a spokesman for the Grand Orange Lodge of Ireland said the institution condemned the content of the video 'without reservation'. The spokesman had said, 'The behaviour of those involved and their actions have no place in our society and certainly do not reflect the ethos of our organisation. If any of those involved are found to be members of the Institution, they will face disciplinary proceedings.'

On the previous day the Grand Secretary of the Orange Order, Mervyn Gibson, had been awarded an MBE in the queen's Jubilee Honours List.

But nationalists on Twitter had points to score. One wrote, 'Sorry but I really think this video should be posted worldwide to show the world the animals in the Orange Order here in the 6 counties. How are we all expected to bring these animals into a New Ireland?'

By the evening two men had apologised for their involvement. They were John Bell and Andrew McDade. In a statement issued through the PA news agency, they said, 'We offer our sincerest and deepest apology to the Harte and McAreavey families, and indeed to wider society for our actions which whilst fuelled by alcohol, can neither be mitigated or excused in any shape or form. Our apology is unequivocal, and our acceptance of wrongdoing is absolute.'

They said also that their family and friends had been subjected to threats and abuse since the video had appeared, that this was unfair since responsibility was theirs alone.

They issued their apology through a consultancy firm run by the loyalist campaigner Jamie Bryson who had himself tweeted his own objections to the video that morning. 'The disgraceful video – mocking the death of a young woman – doing the rounds does not represent unionism or loyalism. It is vile, abhorrent & all those involved should be ashamed, as should those sitting quietly without intervening.'[1]

All sections of unionism expressed the same revulsion but then other tweets came from loyalists arguing that catholics and nationalists had not been similarly prompt in condemning sectarian jokes made from within their community. Where the issue had seemed clear at first, it had evolved into sectarian rivalry with voices on each side of the sectarian divide claiming that those on the other side, all of them, shared a low despicable culture worthy only of condemnation. This is how it works in Northern Ireland.

One tweeter revived a video for which Michaela McAreavey's father, Mickey Harte, had had to apologise, three years earlier. This showed Tyrone GAA supporters on their bus singing IRA songs as they passed an Orange band in Aughnacloy.

While the subject of the song is the murder of Michaela McAreavey, it may be that the target of it, those it most directly intends to offend, are not her family and friends, who would not be personally known to the writer and singers of the song, but the catholic community and the GAA. And even then one has to wonder, for the song may have been around for ten years or more, since the murder and the media coverage, without anyone in that catholic community apparently having heard it. It was not intended to reach them but was recorded by someone in the hall and released through social media. The audience, on this occasion, were the people in the hall, none of whom were likely to have been catholics or members of the GAA. So it appears to have been a rallying song for the loyalists themselves, asserting their right to be sectarian and nasty without actually doing anything about it. In that sense it may be a safety valve to release the hatred that in the past would have culminated in some going out from a bar or a club hall to find a catholic to kill.

Or perhaps it is a football song, written for a cheering crowd of fans to taunt the rival fans and the players for the opposing team on the pitch. Still, it is extraordinary that the song had not emerged into public awareness before that, presumably having been written at a time when the media was covering the murder and the funeral and the trial and acquittal of suspects, years before this.

Linfield Football Club in south Belfast, which draws its support from the protestant community, now apologised for the behaviour of a voluntary worker who had been identified in the video. This was a man who coached young women. The club said he had been removed from his position.

And a company in Craigavon which deals in sand and gravel said it was investigating whether some of its employees had made the video. The company statement said, 'As a family and as a business, we endeavour to ensure an ethos of respect, inclusivity and consideration in everything we do … We will not tolerate or condone sectarianism, bigotry, or intimidation in any form from anyone employed by us.'

So, while the video had shown us protestant bigotry in a disgusting form it had also triggered the rallying of unionist political parties, business and sporting organisations against sectarianism, because a key hurt caused by the song, aside from the distress to the McAreavey family, was letting the side down, disgracing your people.

The defence of Bell and McDade was 'this is not who we are as people'. The widespread condemnation of the video, particularly among loyalists and unionists, emphasised that defence, that it was not representative, that it was an aberration.

Political unionists said they condemned sectarianism. Yet sectarianism drives their vote and holds their movement together. The political party leaders, of course, don't celebrate the murder of Michaela McAreavey and are genuinely appalled by the song and they sent genuine sympathies to the family and sincerely wished that the coarsest elements of their support community would not indulge in hatred and contempt for others. But these parties also work for the coherence and consolidation of that community.

Moore Holmes, who is a loyalist activist, tweeted, 'Loyalists view that video the same way everyone else does – abhorrent. Anyone with a shred of moral decency will find it unsettling. Thankfully, in modern NI, we do not define the mindset of an entire community based on the actions of a few. Those who do only seek to demonise.'[2]

And that sounds fair. But Holmes knows that we do routinely judge whole communities by the actions of a few. Loyalists in the past had seen it as sufficient revenge against the IRA to kill any random catholic. The loyalist paramilitary leader Johnny Adair was filmed in prison with a slogan on his cell wall that said, 'Kill Them All – Let God Sort Them Out'. I doubt that Adair actually knew the papal origins of that slogan. It was coined by the catholic Cistercian abbot Arnaud Amalric, who persecuted the Cathars of southern France in the thirteenth century, in a genocidal crusade ordered by Pope Innocent III.

Judging whole communities by the behaviour of the worst is what sectarianism does. Republicans judge the whole security force apparatus by the actions of a small number of police officers and soldiers who committed murder or covered it up. And it was sectarian to suppose that all those unionists condemning the video were hypocrites who secretly supported it. Or that this one instance proved that songs like this were being sung in Orange halls all over the country.

These sectarian communities both assume a uniformity in each other. And both call their own communities round them in collective support for their cause. Those men singing are part of a spectrum of sectarian feeling that extends from drunken thugs to the more civil antagonism of besuited politicians who seek votes from these same people. That's not to say that everyone on that spectrum is responsible for all of it, but many felt an instant danger of being implicated if they didn't publicly dissociate themselves.

Moore Holmes, saying, in effect, don't judge me by this, is acknowledging that he is part of the community of those men, potentially answerable for them, even if he doesn't actually know them individually, because he operates in that sectarian milieu. He wouldn't fear being judged as like them if he was a catholic nun or a Pakistani shopkeeper or an Alliance Party councillor. He fears being shamed by them because they are loyalists endorsing the same culture, religion and political causes which are important to him too.

In the term used by loyalists, they are both part of what many now call the 'PUL community'. PUL stands for Protestant, Unionist, Loyalist. It presents the whole community and the whole spectrum of religion and politics within it as a collective. They want everyone on 'their side' to be included until they do something so awful that they have to be excluded. And those who like that terminology apply the same treatment to the catholic community by calling it the 'CNR community', Catholic, Nationalist, Republican.

This is thinking that sees society as divided into two comprehensive blocs.

Holmes asks that whole communities aren't judged by the behaviour of a few, but he knows that such judging is precisely what sectarianism is and that loyalism indulges in these generalisations as eagerly as nationalism does. That's why we get graffiti like 'KAT' – 'Kill All Taigs' – and it is also why loyalist energies at election time coalesce into support for unionist parties which are only shamed by them when they so rabidly disgrace themselves.

Undoubtedly many orangemen and unionists were stung by the repeated jibes from nationalists that this showed up what loyalists were really like. And nationalists pointed out that, while this song was particularly nauseating, there are many routine expressions of loyalism, not quite in the same league, but harsh and sectarian, which often do not attract the same outrage. These include annual bonfires on 11 July.

What had roused unionist politicians to leading the way in disowning this song was the degree of malice in it, more than the fact of it. Everyone will take it for granted that loyalists gathering in their halls after a parade will sing outrageous sectarian 'kick-the-pope' songs. The Orange Order pays bands to lead its lodges on parade on the Twelfth and some of those bands celebrate loyalist paramilitary murderers.

It knows that it is organically connected to ribald sectarianism, yet the lodge members march in their sober attire, proud to be decent christians, while the bands thunder before them often beating their drums louder when they pass near catholic streets or a catholic church.

Everyone knows this is how it is. It is inconceivable that the lodges would stop hiring the bands. Some might argue, I suppose, that directing loyalist energies into music making and parading provides an outlet for their anger and communal pride that might otherwise express itself more destructively.

But the vicious sneering at a murder victim and her husband was going too far. And the worrying part of it was that the song had been written down, learnt off by heart, shared with others and sung with enthusiasm eleven years after Michaela's death, which suggested that it had been sung before, perhaps many times in many places.

But does that make hypocrites of the unionists who condemned the song? Were they all as unfamiliar with it as their outrage implied?

I would say that rallying your political energies exclusively from one community in opposition to those who rally theirs from another community is always going to seem to the most thuggish and ignorant among you to endorse raw hatred and violence, particularly when both these cultures have histories of violence that they cherish as legacies.

Loyalism's heroes include savage sectarian terrorists, and republicanism's heroes, honoured by the highest-ranking politicians, include murderers too. If the violent people of the past are absolved in the present, it's natural that present-day followers of these movements will feel entitled to hate and to attack.

And if sectarian communities embrace churches and sporting bodies, schools and clubs and marching bands and political parties, then all will be likely targets from the other side. Michaela McAreavey, to the person who wrote that song, represented Gaelic sport and catholic faith. And the songwriter did not need to theorise about why she should be despised but took joy in her having been killed without even having to think about it. He had probably understood since he was a child who the enemy was.

Or as Moore Holmes himself put it in a later tweet, 'We are familiar with a herd-hate mentality in NI but that video stoops to a new & pitiful low.'[3]

Some read optimistically the rallying of unionists and loyalists in protest against the singing of the cruel song. Keith Duggan in *The Irish Times* wrote, 'The instant outpouring of revulsion at representative and public level across Northern Ireland demonstrated once again that the place is on the verge of a new time. It is an instinctive repudiation of a reprehensible rendition of tired, inherited hatreds.'[4]

This may be partly right. Sectarianism is, hopefully, in decline. But in a sectarian society divided as deeply as Northern Ireland is, from the level of the street to high politics, everything has a sectarian context, even the condemnation of sectarianism.

Some loyalists were tweeting with the hashtag #notinmyname. If I had done that, it would have been seen as entirely beside the point. No one is going to hold me accountable for the behaviour of orangemen because I am of the other community. I would never have been in that hall that night.

The loyalists who dissociated themselves from those in the hall who were singing or cheering felt they had to do so in a way that I did not feel and did not need to feel, because they are part of that community, vulnerable to the catholic community charge that they are all the same. They were the ones who needed to make the case that they were not all the same.

As for the hope that the condemnation of the song was an effective rallying of unionists and nationalists, that is not the full picture. Many nationalists were using the event to attack all of Orangeism and loyalism as having been exposed as uniformly toxic and vicious. This was a sectarian opportunity for them.

This is not to say that individual unionists and loyalists were not genuinely appalled and in sympathy with the Harte and McAreavey families. This is not about individuals, unless it is about the individuals who sang and cheered the song. It is about society and politics.

Social media campaigners did make it about individuals by seeking out the people who were in the hall to publish their names. There would be no forgiving them. Bell and McDade had said, 'this is not who we are as people', meaning, I think, this is not what protestants are like; don't judge others by what we did; this is personal not societal. But the opportunity was there not just to seek out and humiliate those men but to hold them accountable for all protestant sectarianism, to make them forever the most potent symbols of it while affirming, or claiming too, that catholic sectarianism is a myth, catholics being loving and decent people who would never do such a thing.

Sinn Féin's deputy leader Michelle O'Neill, who had often participated in ceremonies honouring IRA killers, said she has spoken to Michaela McAreavey's husband, John, now remarried, 'to offer solidarity to both the McAreavey and Harte families'. She said, 'Hate and sectarianism have no place in our society. People deserve better. Love over hate will always win out.' This had not been the previous policy of Provisional republicans. IRA bomber Thomas Begley had not gone into the fishmonger's on the Shankill to offer hugs to the nine people he killed.

O'Neill had not found Jesus but a propaganda opportunity.

4

What's God Got to Do with It?

Opposing communities in Northern Ireland are homogeneously catholic and protestant. Their leaders may say that they are not in contention about religion and, in fact, the substance of their disputes may almost never be about theological differences. But it is hard to ignore or discount the fact that practically all the people on either one side of a peace wall will have been baptised into the same church or broad denomination, the Catholic Church on one side, a range of Protestant churches and congregations on the other.

The historic figureheads of the opposing sects in Ireland have been the pope and the British monarch. 'FTP' or 'Fuck The Pope' is a common item of graffiti in protestant areas, as is the image of the crown. The writing on the wall says things like 'One Faith, One Crown, No Pope in Our Town'.

Even some who believed very strongly during the early

Troubles that this was a clash of religions see church affiliation as of less relevance today. Wallace Thompson says now, 'That would have been the view in the fifties and sixties. And when the Troubles broke out we became more aware in our own hearts and minds that this was an attack by the power of Rome against us and all our fears were being realised in the IRA campaign. And I would have imbibed that view, that Northern Ireland was separate from the rest of Ireland because of its protestant view, its British perspective.'

As a catholic child of the same generation as Wallace Thompson, I would have been conditioned culturally in an aversion to the British monarchy. Going to Finaghy to watch films in the Tivoli I would hurry to the exit with my friends before the anthem.

In my catholic nationalist upbringing there were lots of little routines, hardly acknowledged, which expressed our disdain for the queen and for England. Like timing Christmas dinner to coincide with the queen's Christmas message on TV so that we wouldn't see it.

In later life, being cool enough to be indifferent to it, I have left it on and watched others dive for the remote.

After the death of Queen Elizabeth II in September 2022 I realised that some of my protestant friends retained some acculturation into reverence for monarchy, while my generation of Northern Irish catholics assimilated easily an understanding that we should hold it in contempt. Conditioning? I believe

I have well-reasoned and rational arguments to support my opposition to monarchy as a thinking adult, but I look around and see that arguments for and against it are coming from separate communities. We may speak with reason and conviction but we also speak as we might have been predicted to, consistent with the prejudices we were nurtured in.

Dr Órfhlaith Campbell tweeted, 'Highlighting that the Queen was the head of a system of colonisation is not sectarian … The implication that we cannot mention this in NI for being sectarian to our neighbours also has some problematic connotations you might want to think about…'[1]

I agree with this, though Queen Elizabeth's was the period in which the empire fell apart. She was really the head of a system of decolonisation.

In protestant households there was none of our perpetual alertness, this self-inoculation against the emotional appeal of monarchy and its rituals. My protestant friends stood for the anthem. They had a picture of the queen on the wall at school. They marked her birthdays and other occasions at school assembly. They respected the flag and even if they didn't want to watch the queen's Christmas message themselves they knew they should be quiet and let their mothers and grannies watch it.

King Charles has sworn to uphold the protestant faith. Catholics aren't taking that too much to heart these days, though it is clearly a direct legacy of the religious wars that established the sectarian division which survives still in Northern Ireland.

The 'No Pope Here' graffiti shows that protestants who want to needle catholics assume that they still identify as much with the papacy as they themselves do with the monarchy. Catholics don't. At least they don't think they do; they have not been tested in the same way that the British have, with the death of their symbolic figure after her having been in place for seventy years, something that no pope could ever match since all are appointed in old age.

But let's try a thought experiment.

Queen Elizabeth is acknowledged to have fostered reconciliation in Northern Ireland. Throughout the Troubles she made little difference because when she visited Northern Ireland it was always to reassure the protestant community of their place in her affections. Peter Robinson, a founder member of the DUP, said her visits had become predictable, after every political setback for unionism, to affirm that they were still British and in her affections.

A change came in 2011 when she visited Dublin for the first time and bowed before a memorial to the republican dead and later when she shook hands with the IRA leader Martin McGuinness in his role as deputy first minister.

In 1979 Pope John Paul II visited Ireland but did not travel north. He pleaded with the IRA to end the violence and this had no effect. Later he sent an emissary to the IRA hunger strikers in the Maze Prison to urge them to come off their fast. They politely ignored him.

But what if he had been able to go to unionists and assure them of his respect? He probably could not have done that. His position as head of the Catholic Church and spiritual leader of the catholics of Northern Ireland has strangely meant more to protestants than to catholics. They had elevated him in importance, reviled him, absurdly, as the guiding hand behind the IRA. And many of their own spiritual leaders would have protested against him while some of the softer anglican churchmen would have met him.

Yet, perhaps there was something he could have done that would have undermined the whole sectarian culture. He could have made a plain statement that he was not and had no wish to be thought an icon of Gaelic republican Ireland, and that he also had no interest in whether or not Ireland was ever united. He could have removed himself from the old quarrel as the queen did on her Dublin visit.

Wallace Thompson actively campaigned against Pope Francis coming to Northern Ireland on a visit to Ireland in 2018 and criticised protestant clergy who had expressed a hope that he might.

Wallace said, 'The issues outlined by Martin Luther 500 years ago have not gone away, they are still there and are every bit as significant now as they were back then. So would it not be better for these Protestant church leaders to seek to proclaim the reformed truth and promote that rather than pandering to the head of a church with whose teachings they should not be in agreement?'[2]

Thompson was not arguing for holy war or endorsing sectarian violence in any way but he was saying plainly that the centuries-old division between catholics and protestants was worth maintaining. He does not see himself as sectarian but he does understand that his religious convictions will alienate catholics from his arguments in defence of the Union.

He tells me, 'The tension for the likes of myself is that I want to uphold the evangelical protestant values, but also if I want to reach out to roman catholics and convince them of the value of the Union, some of the things that I might say in defence of my faith will rankle and cause a problem then for the broader agenda.'

Pope Francis visited Ireland as part of a World Meeting of Families, and in anticipation of the visit there had again been much speculation that he would cross the border. A diplomat confided to me at the time that there had been some hope of the queen and the pope meeting in Belfast to symbolise reconciliation and the end of the old religious war.

When the queen came to honour republicans in Dublin she was saying, in effect, I am not part of this. Count me out of the old squabble; unionists can't diminish the Irish republican tradition in my name. A pope similarly removing himself emphatically from the symbolic role accorded to him by protestant loyalists might similarly have complicated the simple sectarianism of those who still imagined that Rome was the ultimate problem.

In fact, the queen had already met a succession of popes in Rome during her reign, but a public display of amity between a pope and a British monarch in Belfast may well have been a powerful symbol, at least, of a refusal of either to be appropriated as icons by the sectarian factions.

However, the pope is no longer seen as a symbol of their cause by catholics in Northern Ireland, though some protestants have failed to catch on to that. When Francis did come, the numbers who turned out to see him were much lower than those who had gone to see John Paul II in 1979, a clear sign of the waning of catholic religious enthusiasm and an increasing cynicism about the institutional Church.

The origins of division in Northern Ireland lie in the Plantation of Ulster by King James I in the seventeenth century. Protestant England had moved Scottish peasants over to Ulster and given them land among catholic Gaelic neighbours. Privilege was determined by religious affiliation so privilege was at the heart of contention.

When Henry VIII had confronted the papacy, a theological question was his ostensible concern: whether a catholic might divorce and save himself the trouble of beheading his wife before taking a new one. But he was challenging power and asserting his own. The papacy at that time exercised control over much of Europe and could mobilise an army, so the theological question of divorce was also a dispute over how the pope might influence succession to the English throne.

Were the wars that followed 'holy wars' or just more fighting for territory and influence?

It would be impossible to make a clear distinction between a simple intelligible secular motive like the preservation, or expansion, of power and a purely theological motive. Some people entering into such wars no doubt have strong religious motivation, but I doubt whether such wars would be fought at all if at heart they were not about power too.

Religion may then be a tool in such wars, whether to control people on one's own side or to irritate those on the other.

When I was a boy I was brought to the cathedral in Drogheda to see the head of Oliver Plunkett, who became archbishop of Armagh in 1669. My indistinct memory tells me there was blackened skin on the skull and that the skull itself had seemed shrunken. It was displayed inside a glass cube.

Plunkett had been of the old Anglo-Irish aristocracy, itself divided by the religious wars of the seventeenth century. He was out of Ireland, in Rome, when Oliver Cromwell was sacking Drogheda and crushing catholic assertion in Ireland. He lived through a relaxation of the penal laws against catholics, returned to Ireland and then got caught up in a catholic revival, which worried England.

Though unlikely to have been conspiring against the throne, he was tried and executed, hanged, drawn and quartered at Tyburn on 1 July 1681 at the age of fifty-five. His body parts were buried separately in two boxes, presumably to complicate the prospects of resurrection. The wizened head that I had seen on the altar in Drogheda was later brought to Rome and from there to Armagh and then Drogheda.

Plunkett had been found guilty of 'promoting the Roman faith'. Condemning him to death, Lord Chief Justice Sir Francis Pemberton said, 'You have done as much as you could to dishonour God in this case; for the bottom of your treason was your setting up your false religion, than which there is not any thing more displeasing to God, or more pernicious to mankind in the world.'

The expressed reason why Plunkett had to die was that he was spreading the catholic faith. Would he have been martyred for his faith alone if the English had not, at the time, been on alert to the danger of invasion by catholic France? There had already been, in his lifetime, a relaxation of the penal laws, as there would be again when fears of war receded.

Holy war is always about land. When God gave the land of Israel to his chosen people he sent them to take that land away from the Philistines. Does this story really start with God's gift to the jews or is it a myth to rationalise invasion and slaughter? Such myths also serve to bind a people together in a coherent shared imagined identity with each other, usually in opposition to others who cherish other myths.

In modern Israel violation of holy sites like the Temple Mount and the Wailing Wall is regarded as particularly offensive so we find it easier to think of fighting there as having a religious foundation. But insulting someone's religion may be a handy provocation for someone who has other motives in mind. When Israel chose to cede Gaza it decided on pragmatic grounds to remove jewish settlers. Those settlers may have believed that they were merely holding land granted to them by God, but their faith counted for little when a deal had to be made.

The huge outburst of sectarian slaughter that followed the partition of India in 1947 involved religious sensibilities but it was all about land and who occupied it. Millions fled their homes to cross into the country they felt they would be safer in.

Yet, why should land be either muslim or hindu unless people identified so strongly with their religious tradition and felt so bonded together by it that they felt entitled to hold territory in its name to the exclusion of others? So which comes first, religion or land?

Saeed Naqvi in *Being the Other*, writing about life in India before partition, describes a country in which the distinction between muslim and hindu had not sharpened. India was already divided on caste lines to the extent that casteism had permeated Islam there too, so history might have taken another direction to endorse territorial claims by the lower castes, or by the sikhs. There is, in fact, a Khalistan movement which holds that the Punjab should be an independent sikh state.

Naqvi accuses the Congress Party of colluding in exacerbating the division between muslim and hindu. By this analysis, sectarianism is fostered for a political motivation, much as republicans have claimed it was done in Northern Ireland.

The understanding in the Irish republican tradition is that division between catholics and protestants was generated and fostered by the British. You often hear it said, 'They've sown division wherever they have gone. Divide and conquer is their way.' Simplistic as that seems, there is no doubt that some powers have sought to strengthen themselves by playing on the rifts within a society.

The current Indian prime minister Narendra Modi is widely accused of stimulating sectarian violence. Hindu extremists have now taken to challenging the location of mosques on sites which they claim were originally hindu temples. The most famous case of this is the Babri Masjid, a mosque in Ayodhya in Uttar Pradesh, regarded as the birthplace of Lord Rama, an incarnation of Vishnu. The mosque was destroyed by a mob which rallied at the site in December 1992.

The Indian Supreme Court later ruled that a hindu temple should indeed be built on the land and that the government should allocate a different plot of land for a new mosque to replace the one destroyed.

Since then the movement to challenge mosques has extended its reach. I have heard people claim that the Taj Mahal should be destroyed so that the hindu temple they allege was previously on that site might be restored and that the Black Stone in the wall of the Great Mosque at Mecca, venerated by muslims as having been given to Adam, was actually a Shiva lingam.

To understand what is going on here you have to infer motivations in the main actors. Is it a crass type of electioneering by hindus who want to preserve Modi in power? Even so, it can only work if there are others who are deeply affronted by the thought that a mosque may have replaced a temple hundreds of years ago. But even for them, is it about their deep sense of the sanctity of the place or just annoyance that a rival community has scored a point against them?

We don't get this sort of squabbling over holy sites in Ireland. The nearest we have come to it is protest by supporters of the Orange Order that they are entitled to access to 'traditional routes' for their parades, despite the population along the way now being largely catholic. And there was a protestant, Orange-inspired picket for years of a catholic church in Harryville, Ballymena, a mostly protestant area. But actual contention over holy ground doesn't arise. There are shrines, grottos and holy wells all over the country that are left entirely undisturbed, though according to protestant theology they would be classed as heretical. The patron saint of Ireland, St

Patrick, is presumed to be buried in the grounds of a protestant church, Down Cathedral, but no catholic movement insists on tearing down the cathedral and reclaiming the land.

Indeed, to extend the comparison with the Babri Masjid, the cathedral itself stands on land that housed a Benedictine monastery built in the twelfth century. When Henry VIII dissolved the monasteries the Benedictine monastery in Downpatrick fell into disrepair and then in 1609 James I issued a royal charter for a cathedral there. This historic injustice is of no apparent concern to anybody in Ireland today. The cathedral even boasts the Benedictine connection on its website as evidence of a continuity of christian worship on the site.

The ingredients of holy war are definable communities which identify themselves differently from each other according to religion, susceptibility to offence between them and a power differential which tempts one to usurp the other. And clearly for a holy war to proceed there will have to be some who take their religion seriously enough to kill for it, even if they are being manipulated by cynical leaders who have no actual faith.

In Northern Ireland we have rival ethnic communities which are not as religious as they used to be. We have had charismatic religious preachers who stoked up inter-communal strife and it is not beyond imagining that another might emerge. There is no such figure at work today. The last was the Rev. Ian Paisley, co-founder of the Democratic Unionist Party and later a first minister of Northern Ireland in a power sharing executive alongside Sinn Féin. He had moderated his position to the extent that he was able to form a good-humoured partnership with IRA leader Martin McGuinness.

Paisley is an interesting example of the tension between a religious motivation and a grasp for power. He was ultimately disowned by the Free Presbyterian Church, which he founded, because of his political compromises. This raises the suspicion that his primary interest all along was in gaining power rather than in promoting a religious vision.

I first became aware of him not when he was protesting against the Catholic Church but against the anglican bishop of Ripon for his ecumenism. Ecumenism, the effort of Christian Churches to find common ground, was the greatest evil of our time, according to Paisley.

As in nationalism and republicanism, much protest was aimed at consolidating the community more than at opposing the other. Paisley wanted to be the spokesman for a protestant unionist movement that linked religion and politics and that opposed a united Ireland on the grounds that it would be a catholic state. Other unionists might be softer on that line. Some had been born in the South, had family relations there, perhaps with cousins married to catholics. The unionist working-class electorate expected them to be sound on the core issues, that Ulster (meaning Northern Ireland) was protestant, that the Catholic Church was the enemy and that the Irish Republic wanted to capture the North to bring it under the control of the Catholic Church.

These ideas seem bizarre now, just a few decades later, but a unionist leader who seemed soft on them during the period of the Troubles would be attacked by Paisley as a milksop and a weakling and a Lundy. Lundy was the traitor who had exposed Londonderry to invasion in 1689, and his effigy is still burnt there every year by loyalists of an order called the Apprentice Boys after the apprentices who closed the gate against the army of James II.

Paisley was, however, I believe, genuinely devout and sincere in the teachings he promoted, unlike some other preachers who I regard as having been charlatans. I worked in religious affairs journalism in Belfast and met these people and interviewed them many times. Paisley always, before an interview, would remind me that he saw it as his duty to offer me the prospect of salvation. He was civil in his dealings with me when I declined it.

He would say, 'I would not pass a burning house without being roused to concern for those who might be inside, and a young man like you, bent on perdition, rouses the same concern in my heart for your welfare and salvation.' Or something like that. 'But you have declined so let us proceed.'

Paisley was a large, impressive presence with a gift for oratory and he must have been led in some measure by his personality. Had he been a devout believer with the same convictions but without that natural eloquence and a forum in which to refine it, he would never have rallied hundreds of thousands behind him. He went from being a rabble rouser in the sixties, with no political party backing him, to being the unionist who commanded the largest vote of any politician here in the European Parliament elections.

And people who knew him have spoken about his gifts as God-given. I interviewed a follower who believed that a problem that Margaret Thatcher developed in her hand was the result of a curse called down by Paisley on the hand that had signed the Anglo-Irish Agreement of 1985.

So none of this works if people are not impressionable, amenable to being persuaded sufficiently of pure nonsense to be ready to bond together, make sacrifices and take risks.

Paisley taught that the IRA was threatening to draw Ulster under the power of the Roman Catholic Church. He said that the pope was the anti-Christ, the Harlot. This fitted with a gentler religious tradition in Northern Ireland and Scotland, evangelical Christianity, which taught that you could only be saved by a direct personal connection to Jesus through accepting him as your saviour.

There are nice ways of saying that and then there are bloodcurdling, horrific ways of saying it and the latter were the ones that Paisley liked. He favoured biblical quotes that endorsed the distinction of good christians from people who would lead them astray. 'Wherefore come out from among them, and be ye separate, saith the Lord, and touch not the unclean thing; and I will receive you.'

That verse from Corinthians 2, when delivered from a platform outside Belfast City Hall or before a rallying of orangemen, was easily understood as referring to the unclean catholics and encouraging some satisfaction in the understanding that they are all damned to Hell anyway.

The question for now is whether the political ideologies that prevail in Northern Ireland, having grown out of and been strengthened by their past association with opposing christian traditions, will continue to map onto those traditions, or whether the decline of religious practice will erode those foundations and free people to move between the political camps without feeling that they are betraying their communal roots.

There is some weakening in the wall of division.

For my father's generation, Irish republicanism and Catholicism were still intrinsic to each other. The Irish reverence for the martyr made little or no distinction between whether one died for the faith or for the nation. Probably the last wave of enthusiasm for such ideals was the time of the republican hunger strikes in 1981 in which ten men starved themselves to death while demanding that they be regarded as political prisoners, not criminals.

Republican wall murals in catholic areas of Belfast depicted the protesting prisoners praying in their cells, the Virgin Mary standing beside them.

But the Catholic Church was an ardent critic of the IRA campaign. Bishops were excoriating in their condemnation of political murder by the IRA and this in no way restrained the killers or much tempered the popular sympathy for their prison protest. Protestants criticised the Catholic Church for providing funeral rites for IRA terrorists who had been killed while trying to kill others or had died on hunger strike.

At such funerals, local Catholic churches provided the opportunity for supporters and members of the IRA to honour their fallen comrade within the wider community of the dead person's family and circle of friends, amplifying the impression of community endorsement of the IRA campaign. Had churches refused to do this the IRA would have had to organise its own funerals and these might have been much smaller and more conspicuously distasteful.

Republicans sought to impose an onus on the wider catholic community to endorse their cause. This had been one of the main strategies of the IRA hunger strikes in 1981, to make an appeal far beyond the IRA support base by demonstrating the depth of conviction of the men who were prepared to starve and, whether consciously or unconsciously, awakening memories of old ideas of blood sacrifice and catholic martyrdom.

At a church funeral the impression was created that there was no immediate incompatibility between being a supporter of the IRA and a good catholic. Some clergy faced serious criticism for trying to make that distinction.

This is one sectarian driver of division which might have been fixed with a clear determination by the Church that one could not be both a catholic and a member of the IRA or any other terrorist organisation. The Church's defence was that it was not conducting a funeral to endorse or honour the dead but to invite the community to gather to pray for their souls. And there might have been huge community outrage if such a ruling had been made.

Republicans would have argued that if their members were not entitled to a church burial then neither should all sorts of other reviled people, criminals, sex offenders, politicians who had passed unpopular laws.

A new front for confrontation and protest would have opened up and the Church might ultimately have lost.

*

More young people are dissociating themselves from the twin identities. We see this reflected in the growth of the Alliance Party. Where people reject the hold of their communal tradition they tend to move towards supporting non-communalist political parties such as Alliance, the Green Party and People Before Profit.

As for the blocs themselves, they are evolving away from the thinking of the Churches from which they emerged yet, despite secularisation, they remain coherent and distinct. In voting patterns there is negligible crossover between them.

The catholics who now support Sinn Féin and the Social Democratic and Labour Party (SDLP) are less committed to their faith, more liberal in their thinking, less impressed by the authority of a bishop, but they are still mostly people of a catholic background who have come through catholic schools and received the crucial sacraments of the Church.

Even when they campaign and vote for issues like abortion and same-sex marriage which the Catholic Church abhors, they hold together within their parties and show little sign yet of drawing – or even seeking – support from protestants. That is as clear evidence as there could be that theology and church allegiance are not crucial to sectarian self-identification, that faith is not the problem it was, that sectarianism has outgrown it.

The Catholic Church, which was a feared bogeyman of unionists, still has enormous presence, particularly through the catholic schools, but it is not as effective in imposing rules on its people as unionists imagine.

The Church strongly opposes abortion and homosexuality. It provides in canon law for the automatic excommunication of anyone who aids an abortion and describes homosexuality, in one papal encyclical, *Veritatis splendor*, as an 'intrinsic disorder'. None of this impresses the nationalists and republicans who were baptised catholic and educated in catholic schools. They now take more liberal positions on these issues than the Democratic Unionists do. They dissent from their religion more lightly than they dissent from their politics and their sense of community belonging.

Which is not what one would have predicted a generation ago.

Ian Paisley is dead and the Democratic Unionist Party has had to concern itself with the practicalities of government, alongside Sinn Féin. It has retained a moral conservatism that the catholic parties have relaxed. In the eighties the DUP campaigned against the legalisation of homosexuality. In more recent times it opposed the legal facilitation of same-sex marriage and abortion.

Some writers prefer now to refer to those who were raised in the Catholic Church but who reject catholic teaching as 'cultural catholics'. Some terminology is needed to refer to the fact that a community exists of people who were baptised catholic and that two political parties, the SDLP and Sinn Féin, draw almost exclusively on that community for support.

And actual believing catholics who do not support either of these parties would be right to be offended that the term 'catholic', which can properly be applied only to them, is applied to non-believers.

I do not want anyone to call me a cultural catholic and thereby to assume that I am of a massive community of almost half the population and can be assumed to think and react like other cultural catholics. That would be sectarian, to make assumptions about me individually on the basis of my baptism, of which I was oblivious and the schools I wish I had never seen the inside of.

Bureaucracy has come up with the concept of the 'perceived catholics' or 'perceived protestants'. If an official somewhere has decided that I am a perceived catholic, then that is what I am. Sectarian division prevails in Northern Ireland, and the most divisive question between the communities is whether Ireland should be united. Yet all the big Churches are all-Ireland bodies and they answer to assemblies and synods, to elders and bishops and congregations from Cork and Galway to Antrim and Donegal. The Roman Catholic and Church of Ireland primates are based in Armagh but govern parishes north and south. You would expect that broader reach and all-island context to overwhelm narrow and localised factional concerns in the North.

And some southern Irish congregations have not been comfortable with Churches in the North aligning themselves with Orange Order militancy.

In 2003 a Church of Ireland report on opinion within congregations, *The Hard Gospel,* picked up on that unease. The report said that some respondents said that 'The Church's stance towards the constitutional position of Northern Ireland perhaps needs to be further clarified; it may be perceived by some that part of the Church's role should be to defend the union of Northern Ireland with Great Britain.'

The early Paisley would have been apoplectic at the thought that any protestant would doubt that the Church had a responsibility to preserve the Union. After all, wasn't the British monarch the head of the Anglican Church?

He would have been more sympathetic with those northern members of the Church who said they felt insecure and potentially threatened by representation from the Republic at the General Synod.

The Presbyterian Church in Ireland has a liberal wing represented by people such as Duncan Morrow whose father helped found the Corrymeela Community in Ballycastle to encourage good relations between the Churches. Duncan has been head of the Community Relations Council and has advised the governments of Northern Ireland and Scotland on the management of sectarianism.

I have known many of these liberals through my work as a journalist in religious affairs for the BBC and I have often been surprised by their humour. At one Presbyterian Church general assembly a speaker was referring to the then education minister and IRA leader Martin McGuinness when there was a clap of thunder right overhead. The entire assembly burst out laughing.

Once I took up a position by the rear door with my microphone, to watch the opening ceremony, hoping to have a word with the moderator afterwards. I hadn't realised that these austere-looking black-robed men would finish by processing around the hall right past me. As they did so, the moderator and the heads of committees, the most senior members of the Church, walking solemnly towards me, each nodded discreetly and said, 'Hello, Malachi' and 'Good to see you, Malachi.'

That would not have happened, I think, at a conference of catholic bishops, who have long been accustomed to being regarded as princes of the Church. There are no princes in the Presbyterian Church. The moderator is elected, not appointed by a remote authority in Rome, or like the archbishop of Canterbury by the monarch.

The Methodist Church, like the Presbyterian, decides everything by conference, though it regards itself still as an offshoot from the Anglican Church and even invites Church of Ireland bishops to bless new clergy. Harold Good, a former president of the Methodist Church, has been an ardent peace maker, a trusted go-between who could deal with governments and paramilitary organisations. He was chosen, along with a catholic priest, Father Alex Reid, to witness the decommissioning of IRA weapons in 2005, but he could hardly be thought of as a representative northern protestant, though symbolically that was the role he played. His forebears are from the South and he has never espoused the identification of Protestantism with unionism.

And there are many other protestant groups who actively seek to uncouple religion and politics. Some of these are evangelical christian groups which may describe themselves as non-denominational. These are often evangelising groups which are eager to have access to catholic and other young people to try to enthuse them with religious devotion.

So these communities are slipping away from their religious foundations, and religious organisations are divesting themselves of any suggestion that they incorporate hard political principles. Yet the sectarian blocs remain, progressively finding other things to disagree on.

5

Who Isn't Sectarian?

Ethnic rivalry in Northern Ireland is expressed primarily through political division. Religious division has been integral to this but the influence of the Churches and their teachings is waning. Religion still matters, though in a reduced proportion, as a driver of sectarian tension.

The political contention between the two ethnic groups concerns itself primarily with the question of whether Northern Ireland should be part of a united Ireland or remain within the United Kingdom. I'm going to argue that the division is even deeper than a political argument. One clear sign of this is that the two political ideologies attach themselves firmly to ethnic groups. In a world in which people expressed rational independent constitutional preferences there would be greater divergence from communal expectations; there would be some protestants arguing for a united Ireland and some catholics arguing for the Union.

But membership of a community comes with a constitutional prescription and diverging from expectation can lead to a person being reviled as a traitor, a turncoat or a 'souper'. The latter insult relates to those catholics who, during the famine of the 1840s, were alleged to have changed religion to 'take the soup' from evangelising aid workers in Protestant Churches.

There are essentially five main political parties in Northern Ireland.

Sinn Féin and the Social Democratic and Labour Party both want a united Ireland. There are differences between them. Sinn Féin honours the IRA campaign as a legitimate struggle for Irish unity. The SDLP opposed that campaign.

Sinn Féin wants to press on for a referendum on unity. The SDLP wants to heal division in Northern Ireland first.

Both parties are almost one hundred per cent catholic. Neither is wholly committed to the Catholic Church. In the last decade both have come to endorse the legalisation of abortion and same-sex marriage.

On the unionist side there is the Democratic Unionist Party and the Ulster Unionist Party (UUP). The DUP is the more militant exponent of protestant community cohesion and the Union. The UUP seeks to be more inclusive and aspires to winning catholic votes.

Both parties are almost exclusively protestant.

Then there is the Alliance Party, which seeks not to take a position on the Union but to nurture a middle ground between these factions with both protestant and catholic members and attracting protestant and catholic votes.

Neither of the catholic or protestant parties will own up to being sectarian. They would indeed regard it as an insult to describe them as such.

Sinn Féin argues that it wants a united Ireland because that would put right an historic wrong. Ireland was colonised by Britain and partitioned after a war for independence. Irish people, it says, had the right to raise arms against Britain for independence. Sinn Féin bypasses the fact that bombing a pub or a bus station isn't so much an act of war against Britain as against people who drink beer or who use public transport. Currently the party accepts the compromise in the Good Friday Agreement but campaigns for an early referendum on unity and urges the British and Irish governments to prepare for it.

The SDLP wants a united Ireland because that would work to the economic advantage of the whole island. It resents the imputation that its nationalism is just what would be expected of Northern Irish catholics, and insists that its nationalism is rational but fails to win many protestants to support it, other than tactically to hold back Sinn Féin.

The Democratic Unionist Party reveres the British monarchy and the imperial tradition and promotes conservative protestant moral social values. The Ulster Unionist Party seeks to represent itself, like the SDLP, as having a pragmatic understanding of what's right for Northern Ireland, and what it thinks is right is continued membership of the United Kingdom.

It would be entirely unfair to single out a member of either the SDLP or the UUP to accuse that person of pursuing identity politics at the expense of what might be for the common good, but the simple fact is, almost all members of both parties vote as their baptismal lines in a sectarian society would predict.

This is also how things have worked in Britain and Ireland, where affiliation to a political party has been passed down through families. It is just a lot less flexible. Traditional Labour voters in the North of England switched to the Conservatives in the 2019 General Election. That sort of thing doesn't happen in Northern Ireland.

The problems these parties wrestle with is always presented as the issue of the day, and it is framed as ideological, or it is the constitution or a religious or social morality concern. It is never said plainly that the problem is the determination of these communities to be distinct from each other and to needle each other.

The tradition of discrimination against catholics in employment was presumably driven by a sense that protestants were more entitled to jobs when work was scarce. The often-told story of catholics being driven out of the shipyard and having bolts thrown at them as they floundered in the lough they had been cast into relates to a time when soldiers were returning from the Great War to the prospect of unemployment. One common protestant perception was that catholics had betrayed Britain through the Easter Rising of 1916 and the subsequent guerrilla campaign, and that jobs should go to those who had been loyal to the crown.

But no defence of discrimination is ever made by anyone in the public sphere.

Privately it is a little different. A friend told me the following story. Her neighbour was complaining that she could not get home heating oil. As she explained the problem it became clear that she had only been getting oil from a supplier who was a member of her Church of Ireland congregation.

This was in a predominantly catholic town. My friend did not think her neighbour was a sectarian bigot motivated by contempt for catholics. But she was giving her custom, where possible, to other protestants, in the hopes of preserving a dwindling protestant community. She was, incidentally, reducing her own opportunities to interact with catholics, reinforcing a social, cultural and religious rift, but that was not her intention.

At least, I feel inclined not to believe that it was. Presumably even a racist if stuck for home heating might give business to a migrant rather than freeze. Why do I attribute a more generous motive to the protestant woman? Probably because she is my friend's friend. She does not shun her catholic neighbours. She does not walk on the other side of the street to avoid them. She would never dream of throwing a brick through anyone's window.

My friend gave her the name of a catholic oil dealer and she called him and got a delivery the following day and was glad of it.

Yet even civility has a sectarian character to it sometimes, as a particular determination not to let the other side have an excuse to speak ill of you. And that civility is expected on occasions. When no unionist politician attended the funeral of Seamus Heaney in 2013 there was a sense in the catholic community that an obvious opportunity had been missed to ease the old tensions.

Previously, as I've shown, there had been that unionist respect for the daughter of Mickey Harte, Michaela McAreavey, murdered in Mauritius on her honeymoon and since mocked in a loyalist song.

Seamus Heaney was a Nobel Prize winning poet, a writer of global stature. Absence from a funeral like that had clearer meaning; it represented a failure among political unionists to take any notice of Heaney's importance. It was also a failure to give any credit to Northern Ireland for having produced such a man. He was seen as belonging to the catholics. This was their grief.

And Heaney was indeed a catholic in the sense that he emerged from a catholic culture, knew its theology and its mores and had a funeral mass in a Catholic church. But he was also an observer of civic decencies in a divided society. In one poem, 'The Other Side', he describes the protestant neighbour staying outside waiting for the catholics inside to finish their recital of the nightly rosary. Jenny McCartney, a writer from a protestant background, described it as 'a masterpiece of tender perception'.[1]

But it still rankled with her that Heaney was probably better known for his caricature of a protestant bigot in 'The Docker', though he left it out of his *Selected Poems*, perhaps recognising the offence.

Jenny is the daughter of Robert McCartney, an ardent unionist who rejected the Good Friday Agreement and opposed devolution. She wrote, 'There was an inexplicable loneliness when he [Heaney] died, the sense of an end to a long conversation, of remembered passions fading. It is good still to have the poems. It all mattered so much, you see, and he understood its weight.'[2]

So it was not as if Heaney had not been appreciated outside the tribe. Protestant clergy attended the funeral. Past and present presidents of Ireland were there as were Bono and Gerry Adams and Michael Longley, a poet who draws much on his father's experience in the British army. Unionist politicians either discussed going and decided against it or they didn't even consider it. It would be hard to say which would have been worse.

But my point is more that they would have been welcomed there. They would have been congratulated on their magnanimity, and that says two things: that this society is so horribly divided that such a gesture would have been marked as exceptional – which it shouldn't be – and also that, despite the rift, an easing of that division was wanted but too difficult to manage.

There are times when sectarian acrimony in Northern Ireland is like the surliness between estranged siblings who would be better off hugging and making up but can't.

At other times it seems almost to be the accepted backdrop. Patrick Shea tells a story which illustrates this in his beautifully written autobiography *Voices and the Sound of Drums.* As the child of a catholic Royal Irish Constabulary man targeted by the IRA he was both a home ruler and a unionist. There is no contradiction in the two. Home rule would have been devolution to the whole of Ireland from Westminster, similar to the current devolution to Northern Ireland which unionists endorse. Shea worked within the Northern Ireland civil service through the decades of Unionist Party majority when the Orange Order had undue influence over the workings of government. His own promotion to the higher ranks of the service was blocked until ministerial veto on appointments was lifted during the period of civil rights agitation and reform.

He describes in his book a lunch with colleagues, back in the fifties, at which the conversation turned to speculation on who might get an appointment that has come available.

Then 'one of the company said, in the most matter-of-fact way: "Of course, Paddy, you being an RC [Roman Catholic], I suppose we can leave your name out of the reckoning."'[3]

Shea says that the speaker was a liberal-minded friend. He was wounded and appalled but he asked himself if he would have spoken up himself if he had been one of the majority, for no one else at the table commented on the obvious injustice. 'I wondered if, throughout the hierarchy of the civil service, when this subject had been mentioned, as it must have been, anyone had ever thumped a table and called for some sort of a stand or protest against such shabby intolerance.'[4]

He says it was in that moment, when the reality of sectarianism had been made plain, that he felt isolated from his friends.

*

The nearest protestant area to the centre of Belfast, and therefore to Broadcasting House where I worked, is Sandy Row, a street and its tributaries adjoining Great Victoria Street. I would not have walked through Sandy Row during the worst of the Troubles, certainly not at night-time. But I wanted to take the measure of sectarian thinking among Belfast people and there was a simple way to do it. I would go to Sandy Row and record a vox pop, stopping people at random and putting the question to them: are you sectarian?

Then I would walk over to Castle Street where everyone I stopped would be catholic and I would put the same question to them. I got results I did not anticipate. When I asked protestants if they were sectarian, many admitted frankly that they were. Some would try to excuse that with, 'Well, what do you expect?' or 'Isn't everybody in this God-forsaken town?'

But when I asked catholics I got a different response. They all denied that they were sectarian. So I asked them who is sectarian and they said, 'The protestants. They are the bigots. They are the problem.'

I got a similar answer recently when I put the question to Frankie Quinn. Frankie Quinn had been an IRA gunman, a member of a section that called itself the East Tyrone Brigade. He has served two prison sentences, one in the Irish Republic for possession of a Magnum .357 revolver, a tool with only one purpose, and one, in the North along with four other people, for possession of a thousand pound landmine, a G3 rifle, two AK47s and a revolver. He had served five years for the Magnum when caught as part of a tooled-up active service unit, just six months after his release, and then served another fourteen years. Is he sectarian?

He said he accepts that the division in society precedes the partition of Ireland in 1921 and even the Act of Union in 1800. 'But I believe that religion like racism or homophobia or anything like that is driven to keep us divided.'

By his understanding, sectarianism is a creation of the British and the unionists. Logically, then, catholics can't be sectarian because they don't want a divided society; they don't want partition.

He believes that governments use sectarianism to prevent people uniting into mass movements that might produce popular uprisings against injustice: 'I am not saying it is completely manufactured – but it helps governments to divide people so that they can implement their capitalist strategies … They use religion and racism.'

I asked him if he thinks sectarianism will disappear in the united Ireland he had armed himself to bring about. He takes hope from the experience of the Republic where sectarianism waned, even though protestants there had legitimate grievances against the Catholic Church and its influence over government. His logic is that in a state which did not seek to stimulate sectarianism it would die out.

'I am not saying it is completely manufactured – but it helps governments to divide people so that they can implement their capitalist strategies.'

And does he think the loyalist paramilitaries were more sectarian than the republicans?

'Of course they were. What other enemy had they? Loyalists were used and abused by the crown forces, by MI5, MI6 and the British government and politicians. Loyalism dehumanised a section of the community, that catholic nationalist republican community, which made it easier for them to kill us.

'Yes, there was sectarian murder by the IRA, but there was

not a lot of it. Had people come into a room, let's say, from my experience, if there were three or four volunteers in a room and somebody came in and suggested shooting a protestant, they would be kicked from one end of the room to the other and told to leave. That's not what it's about. And it never was about that.'

He rejects the analysis that traces the roots of violence during the Troubles to an historic division within society. 'It was based on the occupation of this country by a foreign army.'

However, the IRA did actively target protestants several times. They bombed pubs in protestant areas, like the Four Step Inn and the Bayardo Bar on the Shankill Road and killed random civilians there.

And when I put it to Frankie that local protestant part-time soldiers, working on farms or driving buses, were shot dead and blown up by the IRA and that their families perceived that as sectarian, he accuses the British of a deliberate strategy of putting those soldiers in 'the front line', though there was no front line and a soldier working on a family farm would surely not be perceived as being on it if there was.

Republicans cling fast to a conviction that the IRA was not sectarian, that it shot protestant soldiers and police officers and construction workers, not because they were protestant but because they served the security forces. And the fact that most, nearly all, police officers were protestant was evidence of the state being sectarian. Still, there are horrific instances of gratuitous murder that can hardly be explained as anything but sectarian.

Thomas Bullock was a fifty-three-year-old farmer and part-time soldier in the locally recruited Ulster Defence Regiment (UDR). That British army regiment had been set up in 1970 to replace the Ulster Special Constabulary (the B Specials) which was exclusively protestant. Initially catholics joined and there was some hope of a cross-community commitment to security, supporting the British army and a reformed police force. The idea disintegrated, largely because of catholic disaffection with the British army. Bullock's main duties as a part-time soldier were manning checkpoints to protect local businesses from IRA bombers.

IRA men kicked in the front door of his house. First they shot Tom's wife Emily, aged fifty. Then they shot Tom. The last thing he saw on Earth was his wife bleeding to death on the living room floor.

The IRA saw Tom Bullock as a soldier working to obstruct its project, but if that was war it was a war crime to shoot him when he was at home, out of uniform, off duty, unarmed. And even if that could be rationalised, why shoot Emily?

A man who was a UDR officer at the time told me he received a mocking phone call on the morning of the funeral to alert him that he'd need to be at work directing traffic in town because a farmer would be leading 'two bullocks' up through Main Street. The hallmark of sectarianism is the dehumanising of the other, and joking about the murder was a clear indicator of that.

*

Claire Hanna is the SDLP MP for Belfast South and a neighbour of mine. I often chat to her at the garden gate as she returns from dropping off the children at school. Sometimes on an evening walk by the river she will pause panting and sweating in her running gear for a quick chat about the likely outworkings of whatever political crisis is foremost at the time. She is a strong and eloquent woman in her forties. Her ethereal image on her election poster could be a *Vogue* cover but in reality she is much more grounded than that implies.

When I suggest that her party might be regarded as sectarian she looks like she might sweep the head off my shoulders. I could hardly have said anything more offensive. The simple reality is that she and most of her party colleagues and voters are catholic by background but that is not by design, not a condition the party wishes to preserve.

She says, 'I am in a party where regrettably the majority of elected representatives are, if not catholic then of a catholic or perceived catholic background, baptised catholic or at least catholic parents. Recovering catholics. And that is because the community of interest of people who believe in a new Ireland has tended to come from that community, but I don't believe sectarian people have been in that party for a very long time.

'People are actively seeking to make that a community of interest and not a community of people who are baptised.'

She believes that there are proportionately more non-catholics in the party's voter base than among its representatives.

She grew up in an Irish-speaking family in the west of Ireland, where the children were brought together in the evening to say the rosary.

'It wasn't a house that particularly discussed identity but it was a house where the Troubles was going on the radio and TV and honestly my most formative political memory is my dad on his hands and knees crying in front of the TV when the news of the Enniskillen bomb came through. I've never seen anything like it. I was seven.

'They were anti-sectarian. Again they were products of a Belfast of a certain time, but I just don't believe active sectarianism or stereotyping would have been tolerated in the house.'

But she agrees that the SDLP doesn't do enough to attract and promote people from outside the catholic community.

And she doesn't accept the Alliance Party's formula for peace, of simply disregarding the sovereignty question. In effect, it disparages all who have clear views for or against the Union.

'I don't believe that the way to stop this society being divided in two is to create a third community that says we are "other" and we are not like you. I think we want to create an atmosphere where people can be a social democrat who believes in centre left politics and a new Ireland and doesn't have to surrender that so that they don't look like "themuns". I think there is a danger that we fetishise the other [the one who doesn't identify] and that anybody who has views that are a bolder colour than the Alliance Party's yellow isn't progressive or isn't centre, and I am worried about that.'

We were talking just after the May 2022 assembly election in which the vote for the middle-ground Alliance Party, which takes no view on the constitutional question, had increased sharply.

'I look at those election results and I say yay it's a victory for the progressive centre, and I look at people like Clare Bailey of the Green Party that were lost in that wash and I think our politics is poorer if we don't allow diversity within diversity.'

The Alliance Party is regarded as the middle ground in Northern Irish politics and attracts votes from people who are fed up with the old division of catholic nationalists versus protestant unionists. But Claire Hanna insists that the SDLP and the UUP, which do take positions on sovereignty, are entitled to claim a share of the middle ground too. They may be virtually single identity parties but they say they are open to expanding into other communities.

By contrast with Claire, Kellie Armstrong is a catholic from a republican background and an MLA, a member of the legislative assembly, for the Alliance Party. I suggested to her that the Alliance Party is still stuck within a sectarian context whether or not it wants to be.

'I don't know other Alliance people's religions, unless they have said it. I know Donnamarie Higgins, who ran in west Belfast, ran there because she lives there. What we have tried to do for years with Alliance is that the area you are representing is one you live close to or you have been involved with for a long time. It doesn't come up. It's not in our selection meetings within the party. We don't ask what anyone is.'

The territorial divisions in Northern Ireland tend to make it likely that Alliance will run a catholic against catholic candidates in the SDLP or Sinn Féin and protestant candidates against unionists, but it doesn't always turn out like that.

The challenge for the Alliance Party will be to hold onto its insistence on not identifying as unionist or nationalist if a referendum is called on a united Ireland. Having brought unionists and nationalists together on the understanding that they don't play identity politics or take sides on the sovereignty question, the party will have to abstain or split.

When I put this to a member who wanted to be anonymous he said, 'I think the party is safe in interpreting its mandate as being against holding a border poll.' In the event of a debate on Irish unity heating up he thinks the party would seek to clarify the problems that unity would create because nationalists are not doing that and unionists are insisting on staying out of such discussions.

'There are other parties that people can vote for if they think that constitutional change is a topic that needs to be addressed as a matter of priority.' An irony there is that their supporters' votes will be needed to decide the issue because neither the nationalist nor unionist parties can combine to deliver the required 50 per cent plus one votes required to decide the issue.

My anonymous Alliance source insists that the SDLP and the UUP are sectarian, though they are affronted by the term. He understands and accepts that sectarian language would not be accepted by the party leaderships but that a party which recruits almost exclusively from one community is sectarian.

'I think it is unhelpful for people to point at the SDLP and UUP and say "you are sectarian". But basically, it is true. Of course, if a protestant asks an SDLP MLA for help, they will almost certainly get it; and any member who says "I hate protestants" would be thrown out of the SDLP. But there has to be an explanation why these parties only have members of one community in them. There isn't a sign on the door at HQ saying "Protestants not welcome". The SDLP's party policy is clearly anti-sectarian. But then I remember that every single large corporation in the UK has policies which strictly oppose sexism, homophobia and racism; yet the boardrooms of each of these corporations are dominated by white, straight men. It's not enough to have a policy to be against sectarianism; you have to go deeper, and parties which think that commitment to solving sectarianism starts and ends with a written policy position are not going to do that.'

Some years ago I was chairing a panel discussion at the John Hewitt Summer School in Armagh. One of the panellists was Arlene Foster, then a minister in the Northern Ireland executive and later leader of the DUP. A young man in the audience asked Foster directly when her party was going to take some responsibility for stoking up sectarian divisions. The whole audience applauded, clearly approving the question.

I turned to Foster and saw her flummoxed and bewildered. She had already told the story of her childhood in the Fermanagh countryside, the shooting and wounding of her father by the IRA and the family's need to leave that home for urban security.

Later I was driving home when she rang me. She was deeply upset that she had been called sectarian. 'Is that really what people think of me? Is that what you think of me?'

6

Dividing Issues

Not only are our main political parties drawing on sectarian communities but they are turning rational political contention into sectarian contention. For instance, the debate on Brexit before the 2016 referendum did not need to be a sectarian debate; parties could have aligned along arguments that had nothing to do with sectarian division. This is what had happened in England, and political parties split over the question of whether or not we should leave the European Union.

Political parties in Northern Ireland held together because their communities took sides against each other on that question as they do on most questions.

Brexit became just another one of those things that protestants and catholics disagreed on, with unionist parties being for it and nationalists against it. The only thing that might have been predicted was that they would disagree.

Sinn Féin until then had actually been opposed to the EU but communal solidarity comes first.

In the approach to the assembly election of 2022, unionists were trying to rally their community around opposition to the Northern Ireland Protocol of the Brexit Withdrawal Agreement. Brexit had created the need for a border between the European Union and the UK. There already was such a border, between Northern Ireland and the Republic, but it was an open border in recognition of the rights of Northern Irish people under the Good Friday Agreement to be Irish or British as they chose.

The EU agreed with Ireland that a land border across Ireland would violate the Good Friday Agreement and jeopardise the peace so a Protocol was negotiated that provided border checks instead at Northern Irish ports.

There were broadly two objections to this. One was pragmatic: restraints on the movement of goods would make them more expensive in Northern Ireland. The other was ideological: the imposition of a border in the Irish Sea would detach Northern Ireland a little from the UK and was as much an affront to the British-identifying people in Northern Ireland as a land border would be to those who saw themselves as Irish.

That rejection of the Protocol by unionists who had endorsed the campaign for Brexit has exacerbated division, critics of unionists saying that they have brought their woes upon themselves.

At the start of the election campaign, the DUP, which held the office of first minister, was demanding changes to the Protocol and to the Good Friday Agreement. It was standing alongside the Traditional Unionist Voice party and its sole MLA, Jim Allister, whose language was even more strident than DUP leader Sir Jeffrey Donaldson's. They were sharing their platforms with Jamie Bryson, an energetic activist and social media warrior.

Campaigning against the Protocol, they addressed gatherings of loyalists supported by loyalist bands, effectively making the Protocol a protestant concern.

Unionism monopolised the campaign against the Protocol. In practical terms, this was a concern with no necessary sectarian character to it. Trade with Great Britain had been made more complicated. I saw that myself with some products becoming unavailable, new paperwork with even small imports like books, delays and an apparent increase in the number of items for sale through online retailers which could not be shipped to Northern Ireland. Had someone without other political baggage shown me a petition urging reform of the Protocol I might well have signed it. But the campaign expressed itself through public rallies around Northern Ireland organised with the help of the Orange Order and with loyalist bands leading marches through protestant areas and towns. It was as if the campaign did not want my support.

The Protocol also facilitated trade between Northern Ireland and the European single market so some business owners were happy with that and believed they would thrive on it. Protestants who took that position, however, were in danger of being reviled within their own communities.

This is what sectarianism does in Northern Ireland; it appropriates issues and associates them with a single community. It turns secular pragmatic concerns into factional issues. Unionists had a further objection to the Protocol, that it effectively altered the Act of Union of 1801 which had required that Ireland be part of the Union with England, Scotland and Wales, trading on the same basis. That Act had been changed many times since, not least by the actual creation of Northern Ireland, something that unionists were widely understood not to have a problem with.

Polling shows that many in the catholic community and in the middle ground do want the Union with Britain to continue. Yet unionist parties show no sign of being able to extend their reach beyond protestant communities to cultivate some of that catholic and agnostic amenability. Nationalist parties are similarly unable to break out of catholic communities to absorb what interest some protestants might have in a united Ireland. If unionism had not branded its campaign as a wholly unionist concern, it might have been able to draw secular support. It appears not to have even considered reaching beyond its base.

And protesting alongside the Orange Order gave the campaign more than a politically unionist character; it made it protestant. It created big rallies that few catholics would even feel safe attending. All of this raises the consideration that the political figures involved in this campaign were concerned not just with the Protocol and the Union but with the protestant character of Northern Ireland, or Ulster as speakers called the region, in continuance of a tradition that, a hundred years or more ago, hoped that the whole province of Ulster might be their territory preserved within the UK.

Observations like these, however, are so pedestrian in Northern Ireland that no one bothers to make them or marvel at their oddity, but that fact is symptomatic of the depth of the problem itself. Only someone very naive about the workings of Northern Irish society would say to Sir Jeffrey Donaldson, 'Do you not think you could attract some catholic support for the reform of the Protocol if you didn't allow the protest to be so protestant in character? Have you ever thought of holding some of your rallies in Twinbrook or Andersonstown?'

Donaldson wanted reform of the agreement and radical change to the Protocol. He had already collapsed the executive of the Northern Ireland Assembly by withdrawing his first minister, Paul Givan, and was threatening to refuse to form a new executive after the election if his terms were not met.

UUP leader Doug Beattie was taking a more moderate position, arguing that the Protocol should indeed be changed but that unionists should not pull down the executive and refuse to govern. When a party entitled to share power declined to do so, that required the partner party to withdraw also.

Donaldson refusing to take his post as deputy first minister would deny the first minister's post to the Sinn Féin leader in Stormont, Michelle O'Neill.

Sinn Féin had previously used the same strategy. Ms O'Neill had been health minister in 2017 when Sinn Féin deputy first minister Martin McGuinness resigned and pulled the assembly down for three years.

Allister, Donaldson and Bryson were also urging unionists in the coming election to vote unionist 'all down the card'. This refers to the list system of proportional representation that applies in assembly elections. Each constituency returns five MLAs. Each voter indicates preferences with a number and may vote for every candidate on a polling card, with surplus votes for a winning candidate passing to the second or third preferences of those who voted for that candidate.

So in Northern Ireland assembly elections, my first preference may be for party A but I can also give a vote to parties B and C and all down the card, to every party standing, if I wish. This system theoretically enables me to rise above my sectarianism and extend a little generosity to parties across the divide.

Hardline unionists were saying, in effect, we don't like Doug Beattie and his wishy washy politics but we do want you to vote for him ahead of any other non-unionist candidate. This is sectarian. It says, even if you disagree with a unionist, you should vote for that candidate before giving the vote to another candidate that you might actually agree with on more issues but who is not a unionist.

Unionists would say that is not sectarian, that they are calling for votes for a diverse range of unionists because the Union itself is in peril and saving the Union comes ahead of saving, for instance, the health service, because without the Union the health service will be in even greater despair. And the threat to the Union is the Protocol.

But they always do this. Their entire strategy has been to present themselves as defenders of a Union under threat. They have been saying for a century and more that the Union is imperilled. They have a stronger argument for saying so now because there is some logic in the argument that the Protocol weakens the Union. But as their opponents keep reminding them, it was unionists who wanted Brexit which created the need for a border either in the Irish Sea or across the island of Ireland. So their credibility as reliable custodians of the Union is damaged. And it is not enhanced by calls for unionist unity which seem to prioritise communal/sectarian solidarity over a pragmatic handling of the problem.

Unionist unity is a sectarian concept.

The call for unionist unity is a call to set other political concerns aside for the sake of preserving the integrity of that community, even by voting for people you disagree with on many issues. Some unionists wanted the legalisation of same-sex marriage and the provision of abortion services; others opposed these things vehemently, yet at election time all were urged to vote for a unionist.

Nationalists do not play the same game, at least not in the same way. Sinn Féin does not urge people to vote for the SDLP, which is also a mainly catholic nationalist party. And the SDLP does not ask its followers to give second preference votes to Sinn Féin. But they do not fight each other. They both campaign for votes in the same catholic communities and are therefore intense rivals but they do not conduct themselves like parties that see each other as a threat. So there is a form of nationalist unity in play also.

At the party conference before the election, the SDLP leader Colm Eastwood directed his wrath and contempt primarily at the DUP. The DUP, he said, was responsible for Brexit and for the Protocol and was now whining about conditions that it had created.

And this is all a good strong viable argument against the DUP. But in a sectarian society like Northern Ireland no one thinking of voting for the DUP is going to have a change of heart after hearing Eastwood sneer at them. There are a few constituencies in which a DUP voter might give a second preference vote to the SDLP tactically, to block Sinn Féin, but sneering at the DUP is not going to help secure that vote; it is more likely to jeopardise it.

When I tweeted a comment on Eastwood's attack on the DUP some suggested that the rivalry between the SDLP and Sinn

Féin expresses itself as a contest to see who is more scathing about the unionists. In effect, Eastwood was demonstrating that he is a more ardent unionist basher than Sinn Féin is in an effort to win votes from nationalists.

Throughout the Troubles I was uneasy about this SDLP failure to really tackle Sinn Féin. During the peace process it was the SDLP leader John Hume who had brought Sinn Féin into political negotiations and helped to validate its standing as a party amenable to compromise and able to constrain the IRA, in which many party members were also leading activists.

So, the logic of that strategy compelled the SDLP not to make use of its knowledge of connections between Sinn Féin and the IRA for electoral advantage and thereby jeopardise the peace process and hand a political advantage over Sinn Féin to unionists.

I understood that and marvelled at how, when I sat down with SDLP members at party conferences I was covering as a journalist, they would vent their contempt for Sinn Féin and the IRA in terms they would never use on the record. But surely the peace process is long over.

And competing with a rival over which is the bigger unionist basher is an appeal to the communitarian, to the voter who likes the consolidation of the catholic sectarian faction. Or it is at least a baulking at any risk of dividing that community.

*

Another example of an issue being appropriated by one side when it should reasonably have divided opinion within both communities is the unionist attitude to the British army. Both communities have suffered from heavy-handed crowd control by soldiers, but unionists, being pro-British, rallied moral support even for a soldier charged with attempted murder.

John Cunningham, aged twenty-seven, was nervous of soldiers, naturally enough, and he was not fully evolved mentally, that is, not highly intelligent or astute. The soldiers who trained their guns on him were not to know that, of course. They only knew that he turned and ran when they saw him so they shot him dead.

They were patrolling in Northern Ireland in 1974, during a time of conflict when they had to be alert to IRA snipers attacking them or laying roadside bombs intended for them. They were in an area where the IRA might do that sort of thing.

So was it a reasonable guess that Cunningham was a terrorist?

It was a plausible assumption, but hardly one on which to base a decision to kill him, especially if he was running away and not posing a threat. Many young men in the area were not terrorists. They were catholics, or of catholic lineage.

The lightness with which the decision was taken to kill Cunningham was perhaps more racist than sectarian, if we can stretch the concept of race to covering the distinction between the English and the Irish. I often had soldiers address me in my youth as Paddy or Mick, terms that Northern Irish protestants don't use.

Did they know he was a catholic? Probably. Did it matter to them? Probably not, except in regard to the fact that a catholic was more likely to be a member of the IRA, and a member of the IRA was more likely to be a threat.

Nearly fifty years later, Dennis Hutchings, who fired two shots that day, was tried for attempted murder. He was not charged with murder because it could not be ascertained for certain that it was one of his shots that had caused John Cunningham's death.

A frail old man, he was brought back to Belfast for trial.

That trial was staged against the backdrop of a campaign against the prosecution of former soldiers. As he walked into court each day he was greeted by loyalist, protestant supporters who believed with him that a soldier should not be charged for alleged crimes committed when on service in Northern Ireland decades earlier. This was despite the fact that some of the victims of dubious killings by soldiers were protestants and loyalists.

Republicans were arguing against an amnesty that would have benefited their own criminal activists, some of them still evading the law. Neither community was acting strictly in its own self-interest but each was taking a position opposed to that of the other because that is what they do.

Hutchings was also supported by British politicians of the Conservative Party.

His trial was not completed. He contracted covid-19 and died while the trial was in progress. He was eighty years old.

His funeral was a major public event with army veterans gathered to honour him. Unionist politicians from Northern Ireland travelled to attend the funeral in England. They spoke of their outrage at him having been prosecuted. They paid respect to a soldier who had done his duty and defended his honour with his life.

Those politicians would not agree that they were being sectarian in discounting the value of a trial to bring justice to the killing of John Cunningham and in honouring one of those who had fired on him.

Indeed, almost no one accused them of being sectarian, not even catholics or nationalists in Northern Ireland, and I wonder why. The basic elements of sectarian thinking are there. The case has similarities to many cases highlighted in the USA of black men and women being shot dead by white police officers.

Perhaps nationalists felt that to have accused the unionist supporters of sectarianism would have detracted from the core argument that justice should be served. They had more to gain from accusing unionists of wanting to compromise the law than from merely pointing out their prejudice in action.

The gathering of supporters around the courthouse gates to meet Dennis Hutchings each day of his trial was plainly loyalist and protestant. No nationalist or catholic joined in, though many had served in the British army.

Regardless of the rationale that an individual protester or unionist supporter might make, collectively each community had decided that this was a sectarian issue, that protestants would support Hutchings and catholics would not. No one needed to say this was sectarian because it was so obvious. Yet, within that, as so often, the individual might claim to be acting reasonably and in good conscience.

Soldiers and ex-soldiers and their defenders were more clearly distant from the risk of being labelled sectarian in their defence of Dennis Hutchings. For them, this was not about John Cunningham being catholic. This was about old soldiers sticking together. They had been serving their country and were entitled to be defended by their own country from being hounded in old age for the actions they had taken as young men. They claimed that no similar cases were being taken against old IRA men, that British soldiers were being singled out and that this was not fair.

Stephen McCarthy is a catholic unionist, a rarity in Northern Ireland. He has a softer take on the British army than many of his former neighbours in west Belfast have, though his experience in youth was much the same as theirs.

He says, 'I can recall the whistles and inappropriate comments of squaddies as my mum walked through Beechmount with me toddling along beside her. I know of the terrible things that were done in Derry, Ballymurphy and elsewhere.'

And he is critical of unionists who think all prosecutions of soldiers should stop.

'Unlike many in the unionist community that cannot fathom "their" soldiers being dragged before the courts while IRA retirees have letters of comfort and serve as elected representatives, I am firmly of the belief (as are many of my party colleagues) that if you served here as a professional soldier, bound by the law, and you broke the law, you should face the law.'

He respects the army. He has worked alongside soldiers and found them 'the kindest, most honourable, organised, disciplined and honest people'. He says soldiers can see through the sheer nonsense of those who claim to be loyal in Northern Ireland but who do not have the insights soldiers have gained in wars elsewhere.

'All of which,' he says, 'give them a perspective on Northern Ireland, and unionism, that often makes them more strategic, measured and willing to compromise for the good of everyone here and the future of Northern Ireland's place in the United Kingdom.'

He says, 'I am also aware there are many exceptions to this.' I myself have had mixed dealings with British soldiers in Northern Ireland. In the early days I could contrast their behaviour towards me on the street with the mannered approach taken by army press officers to me as a young journalist. And not all those who stopped me to frisk me for guns or to ask where I was going dealt with me rudely.

In later years, as a writer, I was invited to speak to soldiers on army bases both in Northern Ireland and in Germany. I twice spoke with groups of chaplains and discovered a couple of things in their culture that surprised me. One was that they were entirely ecumenical. They were not at all like the religious pastors I knew in Northern Ireland, some of whom would not have recognised others even as valid christians, but that protestant and catholic pastors would actually fill in for each other, especially when at war.

The other thing I found was a kind of class structure among them. There were working-class pastors and quite refined upper-class ones who insisted on their rank being acknowledged. When one such officer walked into the room all the others stood up as a mark of respect.

I noticed among army groups that they were not agonising about the past in the way that people in Northern Ireland were. They had moved on to other concerns. When I spoke to a group of junior officers about army atrocities in Northern Ireland I expected the angry and defensive response I would have got from their political apologists. They accepted what I said. They had no problem with it. They had discussed it in their own training as they had discussed Bosnia and Iraq, all now behind them.

*

Though two solid sectarian blocs dominate politics in Northern Ireland, a growing number of people are opting out of the tribal thinking characteristic of their background.

They vote for the Alliance Party and for the Green Party, for People Before Profit and for independents. Some also vote for the SDLP and the Ulster Unionist Party, which they regard as less polarised than Sinn Féin and the Democratic Unionist Party.

Doug Beattie's UUP has been trying to appeal across the divide. This makes sense within a list system of voting. He knows that few catholics will give his party a first preference vote, unless tactically, but he can benefit by a third or fourth preference from nationalists who are not as averse to his brand of unionism as they would be to the more evangelical and socially conservative DUP.

These communities have not come from places far apart from each other. The failures of understanding come from wilful separation and to some degree from religious acculturation. Even the differences in language are accentuated to annoy each other. They all speak English as a first language. They create issues to dispute over. If their core grievances over the constitution were resolved they would find other things to argue about. They contend with each other over language, town names, theology, street signs, the constitution, the Middle East conflict, Brexit and the Northern Ireland Protocol, and sport. This is not to say that any individual or grouping is concerned about all of these but all have been and continue to be in dispute between these communities. Who is to say that the presumed central question of sovereignty really is the core dispute which, once settled, would end all the rancour?

The more sectarian football fans see the meeting of Glasgow Celtic and Glasgow Rangers on the pitch as an extension of the conflict at home. That divide will remain even after a united Ireland. Those who enjoy it would not want it to end. I was standing with my wife in a queue outside a Presbyterian church in the centre of Belfast one night to see a play to be staged there about the United Irishmen. Celtic had beaten Rangers that day and a group of lads walking past us took us for protestants and roared at us. 'Celtic, Yay!'

There are genuine differences between the two cultures, but even estranged siblings may accentuate their differences to annoy each other, distinguish themselves. Catholicism and Protestantism have similar differences to those between Hinduism and Islam, for instance in their regard or disdain for icons.

The presumption of the Good Friday Agreement is that two identities require equal respect and recognition. The term coined was 'parity of esteem'. The presumption was that these two identities in Northern Ireland would relax in their wariness of each other if they had a constitutional right to be treated equally. The mistake there is that they do not want to be treated equally. Each wants to be favoured over the other. They have continued to seek out and cultivate areas of disagreement because disagreeing with each other is what they exist to do.

They even compete over which is more interested in equality than the other.

Republicans like Frankie Quinn want British soldiers who killed here to be regarded as criminals but refuse to allow that the IRA killers be regarded as such. Unionists support those soldiers brought to trial as if allowance should be made for them that should not be extended to republicans. Republicans commemorate as martyrs and heroes people who lavishly killed and bombed and spread swathes of grief all round them, yet concede not a single instance in which a British soldier or local police officer has legitimately killed anyone.

It's not about parity of esteem; it's about overtaking the other.

7

Race

Northern Ireland is divided into two communities and they are communities which struggle to name each other. They are not the catholics and the protestants because religion is irrelevant to many people in both communities. They are not even the nationalists and the unionists because many in both communities, identifiably belonging to that community, don't even vote let alone assert allegiance to one state or another.

We have seen that religion is one of the key dividers between communities in Northern Ireland but also that, while religious belief is waning, sectarian division remains deep and disruptive. Another possible model for describing that division is race. Maybe in Northern Ireland we resemble more the racists who are wary of neighbours of different colour. There is no way of distinguishing a catholic or a protestant by skin colour, hair colour, eye colour or any other physical feature, yet it has seemed natural to some to trace the division back to separate origins.

A United States congressman caused offence when he came to Ireland in May 2022 as part of a delegation studying the effects of the Northern Ireland Protocol of the Brexit Withdrawal Agreement. As so often these days, the offence was given through the choice of words used to label people.

Congressman Richard Neal, speaking on an Irish news programme, said he was in Ireland to express his support for the Good Friday Agreement, reminding us of US efforts to assist the framing of that agreement.

He said, 'We were honest brokers along the way, accepting the notion that we would find space for the planter and the Gael to live together.'

This racist thinking complicates division. It reinforces a perception that entrenches sectarianism, extending the real boundaries of sectarian communities to include many beyond them who do not deserve or wish to be thought of as racially different from people they live among. We could help at least to describe the actual scale of the problem by dispensing with such broad, over-inclusive categories.

And the term 'planter' is regarded by protestants as offensive, suggesting that they do not really belong here.

Congressman Neal might instead have said that the agreement sought to find accommodation between nationalists and unionists about how to share the island of Ireland. The usual trick in seeking resolution between groups of people is to define their grievances by the rational arguments they make and to find compromise between them. Distilling those positions back to perceived racial origins is likely to make resolution more difficult because it takes them back to the point at which they are most remote from each other.

It also implicates people, by ethnicity, in the dispute or conflict who may not wish to be part of it at all.

If we were to describe the trouble in Ireland as a war between the Irish and the English, as some might do from a distance, we would be making assumptions about many Irish and British people who feel no hostility to each other and we might even be setting them up for abuse and targeting by others who accepted that definition.

The first problem with the designations planter and Gael is that they are not accurate descriptors of the people divided from each other. 'Planter' refers to the Scottish and English people who were settled in Ireland over four hundred years ago at the time of the Plantations. In the main, these were protestant people settled in a catholic country, and warfare erupted between them over territory and religious affiliation which represented affiliation to power. The Gaels were defeated and their chieftains fled the country in 1607 to seek allegiances with catholic countries in Europe, primarily with Spain.

But over the centuries the homogeneity of the separate Gaelic and planter peoples dissipated. I am nominally a Gael.

My surname, O'Doherty, links me to a Gaelic tribe in Donegal. My mother was an O'Halloran, also a Gaelic name, but her mother was a Lane. She was Irish but living in Plymouth when she met and married my grandfather. My father's mother was a Kerr from Donegal, a native Irish speaker but with a name that is shared by Scots and English.

The names Kerr and Lane can be British but are also possible derivatives from Gaelic. So my matrilineal forebears might be from one line or the other, or a mix of both.

Beyond that, I can't prove nor do I care to prove that I am pure Gael. My Gaelic origin is not something I would fall back on in a political argument. Mr Neal speaks as if it should be.

Even if the descendants of the planters and the Gaels had not intermarried they would still have the right not to have their views on the Union or on Brexit inferred from their surnames. There are numerous Irish nationalists and republicans with planter names. Gerry Adams and John Hume are among them.

And there are unionists with Gaelic names. The name McGuinness is found on both sides of the divide, as is Kelly. Former DUP first minister Arlene Foster was a Kelly before she married, though she traces that back to the Kellys of the Scottish lowlands.

So inferring someone's politics from their ancestry is lazy thinking and it is prejudice, in this case sectarian prejudice. It is widely understood to be bad form.

Still, Neal was making a generalisation about communities of people rather than making direct inferences about individuals, and that can be valid, to a degree. We can say that most people of evident Gaelic extraction in Northern Ireland are content to be called nationalists and that most descended from the planters are equally happy to be called unionists or British. But they are not happy to be called planters because they aren't.

The Plantation of Ulster was over four hundred years ago. The descendants of those people are as native to Ireland or Northern Ireland as the settlers who took land in North America and Australia. To refer to such people as settlers or planters would suggest that they do not fully belong to those places but that their roots are elsewhere.

In North America governments recognise that there are people descended from those who lived on the land before the settlements and colonisation. They refer to them as the First Nations or the Native Americans, paying respect to ethnic distinctions with attendant religious and cultural mores and practices.

So should some people in Ireland be similarly acknowledged to have been here first, the Gaels?

Well, we do not seek distinctive legal recognition, though we do divide ourselves from each other in separate parts of town, or in housing estates. Follow any discussion on social media about Northern Irish political issues and you will soon encounter many people, usually operating under pseudonyms, making claims for Irish ethnic rights or disparaging unionists as 'planters' or 'huns'. I can only guess at why protestants are called 'huns' and assume it is taken from the offensive slang used for Germans. The irony is that the Easter Rising republicans and the later IRA of the forties both sought alliances with Germany, but the modern-day young bigot can't be expected to know that.

When I, using my Gaelic name (anglicised), make a criticism of, say, militant republicanism, I am often excoriated as a 'west brit' or a 'souper'. The 'west brit' was a person living in the Pale, the eastern part of Ireland, whose manners, customs and loyalties were essentially British. The jibe 'souper' alleges that I have 'taken the soup' or sold my birthright. Those who use these slurs against me infer from my name that I am of a bloodline through my father that goes back to the old Gaelic order. From that they infer that I have responsibilities, to proclaim myself Irish, to assert the right of an Irish nation to govern the whole island, to stand by those who made their protests against partition of the island, some of them through sabotage and murder.

They can't really be sure that I'm as much a pure Gael as my name implies, for the female lines, my own and my father's, might be cluttered with genes from all over the Earth. Still, they presume to know where I belong and what I ought to think. For a day or two on social media and on radio talk shows there was a flurry of discussion around Neal's use of 'planter' and 'Gael'. The Ulster Unionist leader Doug Beattie said he found the term 'planter' 'derogatory'.

But others weighed in with a defence of the terms, pointing out that they had been used by former DUP leader Peter Robinson and by the poet John Hewitt.

I suspect that these defences of the terminology, though not fully unpacked anywhere, were grounded on two realities. One is that far more offensive terms are commonly used to describe 'prods and taigs' or 'huns and fenians' in Northern Ireland, so we are probably less likely to take offence at words that roughly reflect an historical reality. At least Gaels are less likely to be annoyed since the terminology actually honours them as the indigenous Irish. It is only the protestants, the alleged 'planters', who are insulted by Neal's language, and Doug Beattie and others who criticised his use of the term qualified their criticism by saying that they are 'thick skinned' and not bothered.

They did not want to be thought oversensitive.

Some of those on social media who defended the use of the terms recalled that two poets, exploring identity, had adopted the labels for themselves. These were John Montague and John Hewitt.

Montague wrote from catholic experience, Hewitt from protestant. They toured Northern Ireland in 1970 with an Arts Council-sponsored pamphlet of their poems called *The Planter and the Gael*. They read in arts centres, hotels and schools.

This was an effort to ease sectarian tensions by drawing out discussion on division.

In a poem called 'The Dead Kingdom', Montague described Ulster as 'a creaking branch'. Hewitt gave out about the 'creed-crazed zealots and the ignorant crowd' in a poem called 'An Ulster Reckoning'.

Both located the problem of contemporary violence in a long history of sectarian hatred.

Timothy Kearney later brought them together for an interview for the magazine *The Crane Bag*.[1] The first thing he asked them was whether the terms 'planter' and 'Gael' were accurate descriptors of their separate identities.

Hewitt said he never called himself a planter normally and nor did people in the community he came from. But he had used the term in the book's title in order to 'make the admission that my people began to colonize'. He said he was trying to let the Gael know where he stood.

So he had already accepted the concept of his people being distinct and having a collective responsibility for division.

Montague said they were trying to make 'some kind of gesture' presumably to bring protestants and catholics together in a single audience. But that had been before the hardening of the violence and he would not do that in the more troubled period in which he was giving this interview in 1980.

When they had more recently tried again to perform under that title they realised that they were, said Montague, 'assuming roles, assuming masks indeed'. When they had been asked bluntly about their identities at a reading in Larne, neither had said he was a planter or a Gael. Hewitt had described himself as 'a rational humanist' and Montague had 'assumed a yoga posture'.

So they had been caught out as not really representing the sectarian positions they were speaking for. They were the nice planter and the nice Gael urging people to eschew violence and get on with each other, and this seemed fake and irrelevant when sectarianism was in the ascendant again.

Montague said, 'our use of the labels planter and Gael cannot be seen outside of our intended exercise in community relations. And that exercise briefly assumed the two terms as limiting masks which it was then hoped would prompt others to examine their identity more deeply. But certainly with the growing deterioration people had lost all desire to play with such terms.'

The poets contested other ways in which language was used to obscure realities.

Montague said he disliked the use of the term 'the troubles', which seemed to imply that the eruption of violence was a disturbance in a more peaceful normality in Northern Ireland. 'What we are talking about is a recurrent disease.'

He gave Hewitt credit for saying in a long poem called *The Colony*, written in 1949, what 'his Protestant people should do', adding, 'But of course they didn't do it and they are not going to do it.' In that poem, Hewitt had specifically identified himself with the planter but said he would like to 'make amends' and to become, with his catholic neighbours, like the goat and ox that 'may graze in the same field'.

I don't like that image at all. It implies two tribes that have almost nothing in common but four legs and a contentment with eating grass. As a metaphor for catholics and protestants it serves only to suggest that they might live in proximity without any interaction or understanding of each other. Surely Hewitt could have come up with a more inspiring image of reconciliation than that.

I knew Hewitt briefly in the last years of his life. He was friendly and helpful and never showed the slightest intimation of sectarian wariness of me or of anyone that I know of, so it puzzles me that he could have coined such an image. Perhaps by the time I knew him he had moved beyond anguishing over his own sectarianism. In his earlier work, some included in *The Planter and the Gael*, he is honestly sharing with his reader his discomfort in living in a divided society.

Hewitt's writing accepts the depth of difference between a native community and an invaded one. He is a native himself, born in Northern Ireland, but not as much at ease with his neighbours as a native should be. He is anguishing about sectarianism and wishing he could help make it go away but it is a fundamental reality. His is a bleak vision.

In the interview he came back again and again in his poetry to the idea that he was attempting to speak for and to his people but he bemoaned the fact that he was more likely to be quoted in *The Irish Times*, published in Dublin, than in the *Belfast Telegraph*, the paper his neighbours read.

Montague and Hewitt were offering themselves as evidence of people rising above sectarianism. This seems to me to have been a naive response to the violence but it was based on an analysis that sectarianism is the fundamental problem. It just seems overambitious to suppose that in not being sectarian oneself, in having a catholic or a protestant friend, one is setting an example, making a difference. And why is that? Because it is not about interpersonal relations. It is about inter-communal relations. The individual can't make much of a difference.

What they had found on their second tour with *The Planter and the Gael* was that the audiences did not accept them as representative of the communities they wished to be identified with and were not going to take any lessons, let alone leadership, from them.

Seamus Heaney also wrote about uneasy dealings with a protestant neighbour. In 'The Other Side' he writes of a protestant neighbour who often quoted the Bible at him and remarked how 'Your side of the house, I believe, / hardly rule by the Book at all.'[2]

He describes how this neighbour, sometimes calling by, would hear the family at the rosary and would patiently wait until after the litany before declaring himself with a knock on the door and 'a casual whistle'.

This poem is about the civilities with which protestant and catholic neighbours, aware of difference, make space for each other, something that would hardly be worth remarking on if the division was not so deep.

And yet I doubt that such civilities are rare or that personal incivilities have ever been the real problem.

My friend Eamonn told me a story. He had applied for a job with a factory in County Down in the sixties. The English manager interviewed him and told him he could start the following week. Later the manager called on him at home and told him that he could not have the job after all. He apologised for not having understood properly the culture of the company he served and that the other workers would not accept a catholic among them. This was close to Christmas and the same manager sent a hamper to Eamonn, knowing that he would need some help.

This story tells me something nuanced about sectarianism. In this case, it wasn't personal. And this was at a time in Northern Ireland before equality legislation, when it was possible for an employer to flagrantly discriminate. Today that employer would be in big trouble and liable to pay substantial compensation to my friend.

Years later I visited Eamonn in a nursing home, shortly before he died, and we went for a walk around the grounds. Another resident passed us, walking the other way. Eamonn pointedly ignored him. 'I never bother with him,' he said, 'he's one of the other sort.' The man was a protestant and therefore Eamonn did not want his friendship.

I thought he had hardened in his attitudes since the day he told me the story about the hapless factory manager who wasn't clued into our local vicious ways. His different stories reflect two different types of sectarianism, one we might call institutional and one personal.

The Metropolitan police officer who regards with suspicion every black man driving a big car is racist in his attitude to black people in general but he may be perfectly relaxed with black neighbours, a black doctor or the distressed Nigerian mother turning to him for help on the street.

Eamonn was stoical about the rules of the factory, even took pride in understanding them better than the manager did. He was as surprised as anyone when he was offered the job. That was out of character with routine expectation. He had nothing against the manager, nor had the manager anything against him.

And what of the shop steward who had said 'we can't have a catholic in here'? Was he leading the bigotry or accommodating it for the sake of a peaceful life? And was it really the whole workforce who didn't want a catholic or just a few troublemakers who were best appeased?

Another friend, also a catholic, worked in a Belfast factory in the eighties. This factory had a mixed workforce. Blatant discrimination had been outlawed by then. This factory was given a Queen's Award for Industry and all members of the workforce got a little blue brooch with a crown on it to wear on their overalls.

My friend says that for the first few weeks all the workers wore the brooch, but catholics were more careless about keeping it after their overalls had been in the wash while the protestants diligently transferred it to their clean overalls. The result was that after a few weeks it was possible to distinguish the protestants from the catholics by the brooch. A gesture which all the workers had been able to take pride in until wash-day had become a marker of sectarian distinction.

After the fuss around Congressman Neal having used the expression 'planter and Gael' *The Irish News* published a cartoon by Ian Knox belittling the whole issue. This depicted a group of loyalists in Ulster flag T-shirts, with the giant cranes of the old shipyard in the background. One of the loyalists was weeping profusely because someone had called him a planter and another, in a rage, was hurling the Montague and Hewitt poems away.

I worked for years with Ian Knox on a BBC politics programme called *Hearts and Minds*. I was one of a group of writers who would take turns at writing and performing a witty sneering response to the politics of the week and Ian would illustrate these with his caricatures. Cartoonists have long had more latitude to be insulting and Ian got away with representations of political players which, had we been able to paraphrase them, we would never have been allowed to broadcast.

This cartoon caused more offence than it might have done because it was reproduced on social media and therefore reached a protestant audience which does not read *The Irish News*. The outrage was so great that the *Nolan Show* on Radio Ulster followed up with a discussion and I was invited to take part.

I did not like the cartoon. A possible defence of it was that it showed up a touchiness about labels among loyalists who were fond of using nasty labels themselves. Perhaps had one of the loyalists in the cartoon been writing 'Taigs Out' or 'FTP' on a wall, the point would have been clearer. As it was, I said that the point seemed to be that one should not take offence at a racist slur.

I said that the problem in Northern Ireland was that we had morning newspapers, *The Irish News* and the *News Letter*, which serve sectarian communities. The editor of *The Irish News* was not pleased and asked Stephen Nolan, the show's presenter, to read out a statement of his objections:

The *Belfast Telegraph* columnist Malachi O'Doherty made a number of direct criticisms of *The Irish News* on the *Nolan Show* on the thirtieth of May culminating in his claim that we and the *News Letter* cater for separate sectarian communities. However, the two titles have a long record of working together on a range of important initiatives in the past. We provided unprecedented joint editorials opposing violence during some of our darkest days. We sought consensus on hugely contentious issues like parading and we linked up to support the fund raising drive which made the children's hospice in North Belfast a reality. There are very few institutions with an evenly balanced audience in our divided society but it is not without significance that according to the most recent independent survey by the TGI research company one *Irish News* reader in every five is not from the catholic tradition.

My point was made. Eighty per cent of readers of *The Irish News* are from the catholic tradition.

Congressman Richard Neal had not intended to reinforce a tired old sectarian trope and trigger a row but that's what happens in a sectarian society: people cause greater offence than they intend because they are so ignorant of the sensibilities of others.

Duncan Morrow, the academic who studies sectarianism and former chair of the Community Relations Council in Northern Ireland, has been consulted by governments on how to address problems arising from sectarian division.

I visited him in the big new University of Ulster building in Belfast.

He told me, 'Sectarianism is part of a pattern that is so imbedded that you don't even notice it. And it's your normal. Sectarianism is one of these words that just disintegrates on contact with anybody being called it. Everybody denies it. So my view is that there is intentional sectarianism – which exists by the way but which is pretty much in a minority and which is played out at a level which has taken leave of any external management.

'Then you have what I'd call consequential sectarianism. You don't in your own mind intend to be sectarian but the consequences are that people end up giving offence.'

People may be affronted and feel discriminated against while those who cause the offence have no sense of being responsible for it.

'For example, the IRA will always say they were not intentionally sectarian but I would say that consequentially they were extremely sectarian.'

He says that even those cautiously alert to sectarianism may inadvertently promote it. 'Sectarian behaviour like, for instance, never going into someone's area because you'd be vulnerable there, then maintains the system it means to attack.'

Duncan was invited by the Scottish government to report on sectarianism in football, a type of sectarianism which extends into Northern Ireland and feeds the division.

'And you go to the football clubs and they will deny till they die that they are sectarian, even though it is as clear as the end of your nose that that is what they thrive on. It struck me that their dilemma is that they are so constructed that their financial model depends on actually stoking this up. The financial model of football in Scotland depends on the Old Firm.'

The Old Firm is the collective name for the rival clubs Glasgow Rangers and Glasgow Celtic, Rangers drawing their support from protestants, Celtic from catholics.

'The Old Firm,' says Duncan, 'depends on this rivalry being more important than life or death. And you never say you hate them, you just stoke it up. And it's not even that the people running it are more bad than anyone else, it's just that that's the model that brings the punters in.'

He thinks Northern Irish newspapers such as *The Irish News* and the *News Letter* operate in a similar way.

8

Stick with Your Own

A sectarian community does not express its prejudice simply by keeping a distance from its neighbouring community; it imposes a pressure on people within to respect that prejudice and not to violate it.

One columnist on *The Irish News* called me to account for failing in my ethnic duty by addressing the Ulster Unionist Party. The UUP had governed Northern Ireland for fifty years, up to 1972, and had discriminated against catholics. Why would any catholic have anything to do with it?

That was the question raised by James Kelly in the paper read by catholics.

Kelly was not an inexperienced journalist or a fanatical militant radical speaking for a minority faction. He was a veteran reporter in old age, having been northern editor of a major Dublin newspaper, the *Irish Independent*.

Glasgow Celtic FC honoured on a gable wall in the catholic Markets area of Belfast.

Gaelic Athletic Association mural in the catholic Markets area.

(*Above*) The protestant Shankill honours the queen on a gable wall.

(*Left*) Memorial to protestant bomb dead.

GREATER SHANKILL COMMUNITY CONGRAT
THE WORLD'S MOST SUCCESSFUL FOOTBALL C

1
EUROPEAN CUP
WINNERS CUP

55
LEAGUE
TITLES

33
SCOTTISH
CUP WINS

(*Above*) While Glasgow Celtic FC takes its support from catholic areas, here in the protestant Shankill the team to support is Rangers.

(*Right*) My local Orange Hall, in an area that is now mixed.

Kevin Lambe and Grainne Tobin, champions of integrated education.

Claire Hanna, SDLP MP for South Belfast.

(*Above*) The Belfast coat of arms with the Irish hound in chains confronting a mythical seahorse.

(*Right*) Nobel prize-winning Irish poet Seamus Heaney was a keen observer of civilities across the sectarian divide.

(*Left*) Sorcha Eastwood, an assembly member for the Alliance party who grew up taking abuse from both sides.

(*Below*) A founder member of the DUP, Wallace Thompson is embarrassed by crass expressions of protestant sectarianism.

The Belfast Peace Line separates protestant and catholic communities.

Shankill Old Boys marching through Belfast to mark the centenary of Northern Ireland.

The way to get both sides to see your graffiti in Belfast is to write it on the mountain.

Simon Lee (*left*), a protestant in the SDLP, and Stephen McCarthy (*right*), a catholic in the Ulster Unionist Party, meeting almost in the middle of the road.

Yet at this time the political parties representing the catholic community had already agreed a power sharing deal with this same unionist party that I was apparently demeaning myself by speaking to. I was somehow contemptible while SDLP leader John Hume and Sinn Féin leader Gerry Adams were not.

This was in 1999, a year after the Good Friday Agreement, twenty-six years after the Ulster Unionist Party had last governed Northern Ireland and when political progress stalled on a refusal by the IRA to decommission weapons. David Trimble, the first minister and leader of the UUP, was struggling to hold his team together and he invited two journalists, Eoghan Harris and me, and an academic, Paul (now Lord) Bew, to speak to his assembly members, essentially, I think, to help him sound out their amenability to compromise.

Kelly wrote – and the paper published – this:

The Unionists must be hard up actually seeking advice in their present predicament and calling *The Sunday Times* Ex Stickie Eoghan Harris, and Taig Malachi O'Doherty, to address them either on the way forward, or backward, as the case may be.

Strange, strange! …

These odd-balls – the blacks call them 'Uncle Toms' – are trotted out as representative RC's [*sic*] at suitable intervals but they represent nobody but themselves.[1]

This is a very good example of in-house bigotry. Eoghan Harris, then a *Sunday Times* columnist, is described as 'Ex-Stickie'. 'Stickie' was slang for a member of the Official IRA and perhaps extended to political sympathisers. Harris was known to have offered political advice to Official republicans, as to many other political groups and movements down the years.

'Taig' is a derogatory word for an Irish catholic, usually used by protestants, and it reads a bit strangely here. One way in which a catholic might use the word is in the term 'token taig', which refers to catholics who allow themselves to be incorporated into protestant projects to dilute their otherwise obvious homogeneity, taking the bad look off protestant sectarianism. Since this is essentially what is implied by Kelly later calling me an 'Uncle Tom', I suspect that this was the original phrase that occurred to him, perhaps trimmed by a sub-editor who was more alert to the law than to the errant apostrophe.

I am accused here of seeking to represent the 'RC's'. Kelly was a brilliant writer. What hurt most about this article was that he had known me in my early years in journalism and helped me get published in Dublin. Having myself been a columnist for *The Irish News* I had met him often and drunk wine and talked politics with him at office Christmas parties.

The RCs are the roman catholics. Kelly imagines himself to be quoting unionist prejudice by using protestant sectarian language. Catholics don't call themselves RCs. He supposes that the unionists who invited me to speak to them looked down on me. He trusts that he understood them better than I did myself.

Kelly's contempt for unionists had grown over years of covering the old Stormont parliament as a political reporter. He remembered how bad things had been and it appalled him that people like me seemed to have forgotten.

What mental acrobatics persuaded them to hang on to the coat-tails of a party led for twenty years by Lord Brookeborough, who told the world that 'he would not have one of them about his place', one can only guess.
Did their da's [*sic*] never tell them how it all began?

Brookeborough's period as prime minister of Northern Ireland ended in 1963, thirty-six years before Kelly wrote his article. He is indeed often quoted as having said that he would not have a catholic about the place and it is on record that he vetoed catholics attaining high office in the civil service. So, no excuses for him.

That someone of Kelly's intelligence and history was so cynical about unionism, and that the largest catholic community newspaper published that article, augured ill for the success of the Good Friday Agreement. Even at a time when a political system was being put in place to try to end discrimination and injustice he was convinced that the old sectarian blocs were still firmly in place and that someone like me who was trying not to be locked into the old ways was a fool.

This is quintessential sectarianism which always looks to the past and always insists that those others have not changed and never will.

He was accusing me of seeking to represent the whole catholic community, which he assumed had a singular coherent position which I had failed to accord with. In fact, I had made no claim to be representing anyone but myself. The fact that I represented only myself is thrown back at me as an insult as if this was a self-evident failing in me, that I presumed to have an individual perspective, a considered independent thought.

This is what sectarianism does.

Kelly did not stop to consider that I had the right to stand alone and air an opinion of my own without first consulting my ancestors, or him.

I complained to the Press Complaints Commission about this article at the time but my point was not understood, that a catholic writer, Kelly, accusing another catholic, me, of reneging on a communal responsibility is sectarian.

If I, a white man, abuse my white neighbour because he consorted with black people, that is racist, even if no black person ever hears about it.

This article of Kelly's fits with a seething prejudice and energetic propaganda that insists on defining Irish people as authentic or inauthentic, calling them back to the 'planter and Gael' distinction, asserting that their political allegiances are predetermined and holding in contempt those who reject this because they undermine that project.

In a much more recent column in *The Irish News*, Brian Feeney argued that sectarian coherence was still so strong that even a small step towards simple majority rule democracy in Northern Ireland was impossible. This referred to a suggestion being developed that a form of voluntary coalition in Stormont might replace the current, highly vulnerable system of mandatory coalition. Under that system, the larger party of either sectarian community can bring down the executive simply by walking out and leaving the larger party elected by the other community without the required partner. This had already happened several times, most notably when Sinn Féin walked out in 2017 and when the DUP refused to form a government after the assembly election of 2022.

The proposed solution to this was that the larger party of one community might be allowed to make a deal with the smaller party of the other, if it hadn't walked out. That would enable cross-community power sharing and secure the executive against collapse.

And since the smaller parties of unionism and nationalism, the Ulster Unionist Party and the SDLP, tend to be more moderate in their demands, such an executive might be more stable than one between the bigger, essentially more sectarian parties.

Feeney said this idea was 'political naiveté'. 'Well dare the minor party of either nationalist or unionist designation join in an executive excluding the representatives of the majority of unionism or nationalism. Catch yourself on.'[2]

It made more sense, by his reasoning, to advance the argument for a referendum on a united Ireland, in which, I presume, he supposes, government would be more stable.

The vision is the same as Kelly's, that nothing changes here and nothing can.

This isn't ostensibly as much of a defence of sectarianism as Kelly's column was. Feeney might be right in claiming that the larger sectarian parties would never allow the smaller parties of their community to govern in coalition and force them into opposition, but note the exultant tone, 'Well dare they. Catch yourself on.' If this is a simply obvious reality then it is one that excites him.

That sectarianism which obliges people to adhere to the presumed values of the community they were born into has attempted to restrain other writers even recently.

Susan McKay had recognised the shock of the death of Queen Elizabeth II within the protestant community. Writing for *The Irish Times* she said, 'The monarch will always mean more in the last colonial outpost than at the heart of empire.'[3]

Northern Ireland isn't actually a colonial outpost. Colonies don't send MPs to the parliament of the imperial power with votes to cast on questions like whether that power should go to war, increase welfare payments or build a railway line between two cities. But that's not my main point here.

The queen's death, said McKay, was, for unionists, an earthquake. She was accused on Twitter of 'obsessive rants' and 'mean spiritedness'.

There were actually much more scathing pieces about Queen Elizabeth on the same day in the same paper, by Fintan O'Toole and Kathy Sheridan.

Kathy Sheridan said of her, 'With rare exceptions, she spent a lifetime saying nothing remotely interesting aloud, yet stepping out hundreds of times a year to greet her bedazzled subjects.'[4]

So why did Susan McKay's piece cause greater offence than Sheridan's and O'Toole's? Surely it was because, as a northern protestant, she was expected to empathise more with the hurt felt in that community. She was being called back into line, denied the right to diverge from the expectations of those she had grown up among.

One who suffered similarly is writer and sociologist Claire Mitchell, a protestant who describes herself as a republican.

She says, 'I wrote something and people didn't like it and they put my home address online and pictures of me and told people to call over to my house and critique my writing. So that was pretty shit and traumatic and I thought I might stop writing for a few months. I want my kids to stay on this island and I think you have to stand up and be counted and so I didn't stop writing. I didn't change what I was saying either I think.'

She says that all of those she worked with for her book *The Ghost Limb: Alternative Protestants and the Spirit of 1798* have been 'lundied', that is, treated as traitors to the protestant unionist tradition they are presumed to owe some loyalty to.

'But we have got to a point where we're fucking sick of it. Is this what you bequeath to your children, this hiding, swallowing it all?'

She says, 'A lot of people with my kind of politics walk around feeling like they are the only one or that there is hardly any of us and we are used to being lundied and learning how to shut up for your own physical safety, and this book was to let people know there are loads of us in so many different subcultures and pockets of contemporary Northern Ireland.'

The Catholic Paper and the Protestant Paper

Northern Ireland's distinct sectarian communities vote for different political parties, go to different churches, live in different areas, support different teams and even types of sport, and they read different newspapers. There is no better indicator of the depth and character of the rift between these communities than the content of those papers which illustrate all the ways in which catholics and protestants separate themselves from each other.

There are three main Northern Ireland daily newspapers: the protestant one, the catholic one and the middling one. These are the *News Letter, The Irish News* and the *Belfast Telegraph*. The *News Letter* and *The Irish News* cater for distinctly different communities with different interests in politics and sport. The *Belfast Telegraph* tries to reach both communities.

You can see these approaches in a single week from 12 March 2022, a week that included St Patrick's Day.

For *The Irish News* the forthcoming Michael Conlan boxing match generated a news story as well as sports page coverage. Conlan was due to face Leigh Wood, the WBA featherweight champion of the world. The story was: Conlan takes flak for pride in being Irish says brother.

Michael Conlan is a young boxer from west Belfast, well loved in his own community and charming in his media performances. You can see in him a brash confidence mixed with some surprise that he has come so far and become so famous.

The background to this story is that Conlan had come to be associated with a song celebrating the IRA. 'Celtic Symphony' by the Wolfe Tones was played as his entrance music at a previous big fight. The song includes the words 'Up the 'Ra', 'the 'Ra' being a slang term for the IRA.

Conlan had taken flak for walking on to that song and he had apologised for it. Still, this had lost him support in the protestant community.

Previous champion boxers, as easily identified as protestant or catholic, such as Barry McGuigan and Carl Frampton, took care to nurture support across the divide. Conlan had not.

He was quoted as saying, 'I'm just a proud Irishman. I've always been honest and up front about who I am. I wouldn't be true to myself if I did hide it. Has it cost me fans? – 100 per cent.'[1]

What had most likely cost him fans was not his being Irish but his implied support for the IRA in the use of that song.

He said, 'They think I am someone who hates protestants and stuff which is completely wrong.'

He was dodging the main point but it wasn't actually being put to him either.

Michael Conlan was on the back page too in the lead sports story. He was pictured with his outstretched arms holding an Irish tricolour behind him and wearing tricoloured spectacles. The report said that he would thrive on the boos he received at the weigh-in, at his first experience of being the 'away fighter'.

'All those boos will be stored up, every insult will give him energy.'[2] Reporter Andy Watters was clearly on his side.

Conlan himself was quoted sneering at his opponent: 'he'll walk into shots all night. I'll destroy Leigh Wood.'

And inside there was a double-page spread including a full-page picture of Conlan, sweating and draped in towelling with a green Celtic interweave pattern. His Irishness was his brand.

The heading was: 'World at His Feet'.

The story there was a profile of a reckless young boxer who had smoked weed and stayed out all night then realised he had to give up drugs when faced with the prospect of failing a test before the Commonwealth Youth Games qualifiers. This was a lad who might have gone astray and wasted his life, but he had been able to discipline himself and shape up as a world-class boxer.

And there was yet another double-page spread in the same paper on Conlan's Date With Destiny. This was clearly, for

Irish News readers, a major sporting event taking up almost five pages. And there is little that is surprising in that. Any newspaper in the world would give huge coverage to a local boy taking a shot at a world title.

But the *News Letter* didn't mention Conlan or the fight at all.

Here was a Belfast man who was a contender for a world championship, and a daily newspaper in his home city was presuming that its protestant readership had no interest in him at all. Nor was it inclined to make any effort to stimulate such interest.

The *Belfast Telegraph* covered the story without any reference to Conlan having branded himself as a militant Irish nationalist. David Kelly's account was an informed appraisal of Conlan's evolution and influences as a boxer.

He said, 'Wood has shown he'll be no pushover but Conlan's burning desire to take the prize, allied to his ring IQ, should get the job done after twelve competitive rounds.'[3]

That was a sound prediction that nearly came true.

Conlan fought well and by the twelfth round was ahead on points. Then, when he was close to the ropes, Wood hit him hard in the head and seemed to knock the off switch. Conlan's arms simply dropped. Then, probably unconscious at that point, he took three more blows to the head and stumbled, backside first through the ropes and into the crowd. The fight was over. He had lost. He was taken on a stretcher from the ring and rushed to hospital for urgent checks for brain damage.

The hopes of *Irish News* readers and his thousands of fans were dashed.

A city poised to cheer slumped back in its seat, deflated.

But the *News Letter* did not report the fight in the next day's edition. It made no mention of it at all.

The Irish News ran a story on page 8 that Conlan wanted a rematch with Wood and a similar story making the same point on the back page. Inside the sports pages it also ran a double-page spread and a round by round account of the fight.

The *Belfast Telegraph* also ran a substantial report of the fight and an inside page news feature with a picture of Conlan with his fiancée and children and quoting another famous Belfast boxer, Carl Frampton, saying the fight was the best he had ever seen.

So the *Belfast Telegraph* was trying to fit Michael Conlan into a tradition of great lovable Northern Irish boxers like McGuigan and Frampton. Each was identifiable as having roots in one or the other community, McGuigan as a catholic and Frampton as a protestant from a loyalist area of Belfast. Each had become an icon of anti-sectarian branding and secured popularity in both communities, which Conlan had not. The *Belfast Telegraph* seemed to be trying to extend that opportunity to him, despite much of the protestant community having already lost interest in him.

There were deficiencies in the ways in which all three papers handled the Conlan story. *The Irish News* was wrong to let him get away with the claim that he had lost popularity simply for being Irish. The *Belfast Telegraph* was wrong to ignore the fact that he had alienated a section of his potential local support. The intention seems benign but perhaps in a sectarian society it is important to highlight the divisive issues rather than cosmetically gloss over them. And the *News Letter*'s decision not to cover a world championship fight in which a local man was a hopeful contender would be regarded by any sports editor as a perverse decision.

That same sectarian division in sports interest was evident also in the coverage that weekend of the Gaelic football match between Dublin and Tyrone and the soccer match between Cliftonville and Coleraine.

On Saturday 12 March *The Irish News* and the *Belfast Telegraph* anticipated the Dublin/Tyrone match. The *News Letter* didn't mention it. Gaelic sport is a catholic community interest.

All three papers gave similarly spaced coverage to the big game between Cliftonville and Coleraine. They reported on the match on Monday and all had follow-up articles on the Tuesday.

The *News Letter* gave the game more coverage, with Henry McDonald, their new political editor, revelling in the achievements of Cliftonville, a team he has supported since childhood. Cliftonville is a team with a predominantly catholic support base so celebration of its victory in the *News Letter* was a heartening change.

None of the reportage or comment made any reference to sectarian chanting by fans of both teams. This would be a big story later in the week, though only in the *Belfast Telegraph*. Those earlier reports had commented on the huge energy of the crowd and the gratitude of the Cliftonville team, but they had conveyed no sense that some of that support was toxic.

Then on St Patrick's Day the *Belfast Telegraph* reported that Jim Boyce, a former FIFA vice president, was calling on politicians on all sides to condemn sectarian chanting at games. Boyce, himself a former Cliftonville chairman, told the *Belfast Telegraph*'s Steven Beacom, 'Unfortunately there are a small section who are causing problems and while I would not like to see stadiums closed, I appreciate that something has to be done about these morons.'[4]

Complaints had been lodged about fans of both teams.

On Tuesday 15 March *The Irish News* and the *Belfast Telegraph* back pages both carried large photographs of Glasgow Celtic players in a match in which they had defeated Dundee United. The *News Letter* ignored this. Support for Glasgow Celtic is perceived as a catholic community interest.

On 17 March, St Patrick's Day, the *Belfast Telegraph* and the *News Letter* carried articles ahead of a Europa League football final that evening in Belgrade in which Glasgow Rangers would face Red Star. The *News Letter* devoted the whole back page to the story with a large photograph of the Rangers manager, Giovanni von Bronckhorst. *The Irish News* gave only the slightest billing to the match, an eight paragraph, down page piece without a photograph.

A casual reader from outside might have assumed that the *News Letter* and *The Irish News* had a similar interest in Scottish football, but *The Irish News* only gets enthusiastic about Glasgow Celtic and the *News Letter* only about Rangers. These are viewed as expressing rival sectarian cultures and the papers clearly take sides in the communal rift. That tells you two things about each paper: they presume that their readers are sectarian, and they have no aspiration to reach readers who are not.

Rugby is assumed by sports editors to be of interest across the sectarian divide. All three papers looked ahead to two big rugby games, the Six Nations clash between Ireland and England and the Ulster/Leinster Game in the United Rugby Championship.

Two out of three papers got excited about the St Patrick's Day Schools' Cup rugby match between Methodist College and Campbell College, both protestant schools. *The Irish News* gave it only about a third of an inside page which led with Ireland's hopes in the Triple Crown.

All of the schools participating in the Schools' Cup are state or private schools with predominantly protestant intakes, though many of those schools now do have catholic pupils so there must be catholic families which take an interest in the progress of the league and the result of the final. There must be middle-class catholic children who would know the main players so the scant coverage in *The Irish News* may have been misjudged. The report was concise and paid due tribute to the best players but it reads almost like an exercise in packing the greatest possible detail into the shortest space, 235 words. This was beside a full-page article about a film on Amazon Prime about the GAA. And in the same issue there was another full-page article about how well Cliftonville had done earlier in the week.

But it is the job of editors to know their market and to give readers what they want so perhaps this level of coverage was based on sound judgement. The *News Letter* on the day after the Schools' Cup match had a photograph of the winning team with the cup prominently placed on the front page, illustrating clearly that the paper saw the match as being of more interest to the protestant community.

My focus here has been on sports coverage but an analysis of political and cultural coverage in the same papers would indicate the same sectarian biases.

The *News Letter*'s coverage of the St Patrick's Day celebration was trailed on the front page with a picture of a child presenting a shamrock to Princess Catherine, Duchess of Cambridge at an Irish Guards ceremony. This is an image which associates the celebration of Irishness with respect for royalty and the British army.

The Irish News made no mention of that event. The *Belfast Telegraph* included it among a range of stories and images of the day's local celebrations in a double-page spread.

Though St Patrick's Day is a holiday for everyone, *The Irish News,* the paper serving the catholic community, gave much more space to it than the others did, roughly double. About a quarter of the front page was devoted to a photograph of three small children playing with a large Irish tricolour, big enough to cover them all. This was the only use of the tricolour image in any of the three papers.

In the past there have been efforts to discourage people from bringing the tricolour to Belfast's St Patrick's Day celebrations. Some council areas have tried to ban the flag from their festivities for fear of alienating protestants who might also wish to take part. *The Irish News* did not apply that consideration to the design of its front page, suggesting it assumes protestants don't read the paper or that it has little interest in attracting them.

I thought that one way in which I might get a clear sense of the religious background of readers would be by studying death notices. This isn't as handy an approach as I'd hoped because one paper, *The Irish News,* carries many more death notices than the others so easy comparisons are not dependable measures.

In that weekend edition of the *News Letter* there were nine death notices. Four of them referenced Protestant churches as funeral venues and five made no reference to religion at all.

In some, the list of names of relatives included both common catholic and protestant names, suggesting intermarriage within the family.

The sample here is far too small to be indicative, yet, if repeated, would suggest that the *News Letter* readership is at least as secular as religious.

The Irish News had many more death notices, seventy-three. Those seventy-three notices covered twenty-four deaths, with few of the deceased getting only one notice and one getting fourteen. Catholics are more inclined to publish notices as tributes rather than just as announcements.

Of the seventy-three notices forty-six were religiously informed, some more than others, only a slighter higher proportion, for what it's worth, than that in the *News Letter*. Those that referred to a church building all named a catholic one. Many went further and included a small prayer to St Anthony, St Jude, St Pio or others. Twenty-seven of the notices were completely secular in tone, though many of these named a Gaelic sports club and used Irish language terms suggesting their origin in a catholic culture but without that still being a devotional culture.

When my mother died in 1987 the undertaker asked me to write the death notice to go in *The Irish News*. I attached no prayer to it but someone else, whether the undertaker managing the notice or the paper itself, added one, presumably feeling that it would have been in bad taste in those days to publish a death notice without some religious character to it. That thinking has clearly expired. These secular notices do not suggest that the people mentioned are not catholics but they do suggest they are not deep religious believers.

Nor does the greater number of notices in *The Irish News* suggest that more catholics are dying. *The Irish News* is famous for its death notices. It has often been joked that older people only buy the paper to see who is dead. Presumably many people who die do not have any notices placed in a paper on their behalf.

There were twenty-two death notices in the *Belfast Telegraph* on the same day, most without any religious content beyond the name of the church at which the funeral service would be held. Only nine of them referred to a church or included a prayer, sometimes just a psalm number.

On other days I saw notices that appeared in both *The Irish News* and the *Belfast Telegraph* with prayers attached.

Another consideration here would have to be that some protestant traditions do not encourage prayers for the dead in the way that the catholic tradition does, so the lack of a prayer in a death notice in the *News Letter* or the *Belfast Telegraph* may not always be indicative of secular thinking but in most cases it probably is. Religious protestants often attached a scriptural reference like Psalm 23 or Phil. 1:22.

The conclusion from the study of death notices must be that both major religious traditions in Northern Ireland are secularising and yet holding together as communities of shared political, cultural and sporting interests.

The big Belfast papers, as we have seen from their news and sports coverage, present themselves as catholic/nationalist, protestant/unionist and secular/middle ground. In Northern Ireland there are several regional newspapers expressing similar divisions and sometimes working to moderate them.

Seamus McFadden, a Strabane newsagent and president of Foyle and District Newsagents Federation, offered me a brief summary of papers he sells. He says that some papers clearly recognise that their community identification hinders sales and try to break out of it to widen their market.

He describes the *Strabane Weekly* as trying to reach out and attract the catholic reader by covering Gaelic sports. The *Londonderry Sentinel* sells one copy in his shop each week to a man who is interested in its cricket coverage.

But, he says, the papers are in decline, many selling only a third of what they used to. The exception is in the rural areas, so rural papers such as the *Fermanagh Herald* and the *Impartial Reporter* still hold up their numbers.

I asked Seamus if sectarianism was a bad marketing strategy. He said, 'To some extent a paper may be losing its identity by trying to please everybody. It might well lose out. It's very hard to have an eclectic mix. You have an Orange parade and then you flick over and see a double-page spread on the GAA. I don't know if that works or not.'

He says, 'I have two catholics who get the *News Letter* every Saturday but it's for the farming supplement. Farming and sport are cutting across the divide. If a paper is seen as the best paper for a particular interest it will sell.'

10

Languages

There is no precise symmetry between the two main sectarian factions in Northern Ireland. It is too easily said that one is as bad as the other. They are so different that there is no clear metric by which their degrees of aversion to each other can be compared. Yet they are shaped in reaction to one another. The anti-Protocol campaign satisfied several traditional unionist gripes and therefore slotted neatly into traditions of suspicion of the Irish government, distrust of Britain and a fear of being outflanked in an inter-communal competition.

On the catholic nationalist side there was a campaign for an Irish language act. This became a counterpoint to the unionist campaign over the Protocol, not just contemporaneous with it but coupled with it.

In 2017, Sinn Féin brought down the power sharing executive by resigning from it. This was a protest against then

DUP leader Arlene Foster refusing to resign to allow for an inquiry into a hugely expensive and badly managed renewable heating scheme. The assembly was inactive for three years, not because of the heating scheme debacle but because Sinn Féin set as the price of its return an Irish language act which had been agreed to in 2006 but not implemented.

The Irish language was the old Gaelic language of the Irish and had almost died out except in rural areas of the west of Ireland. Some say it was killed off by the British. Others read the decline more benignly as a natural evolution when it became more practical to speak English in order to find work and to conduct trade.

The first major effort to revive the language in the nineteenth century was actually led by protestants of the old Anglo-Irish tradition, the landed classes. After the war of independence the government of the Free State determined that the language should be the official language and be mandatory in schools, in the hope that within a generation it would be the primary spoken language in the country. This effort failed but it established a firm linkage between promotion of the language and the cause of Irish independence.

My grandmother on my father's side was a native speaker, according to the census records. I never heard my father speak a word of it, though he had a colloquial English which included a vocabulary that many modern English people would not be familiar with.

Unionists have met the demand for the elevation of the Irish language with a counter-demand for recognition of Ulster Scots. That is the name they gave to that dialect my father spoke. And he was the son of a native Irish-speaking mother. There was no logic or basis in history, demography or culture for the separation of these ways of speaking into protestant and catholic camps.

I learnt Irish at school from the Christian Brothers, who linked it with the nationalist aspiration. Ireland, they said, could not ever be a free nation like France or Germany if it still spoke the language of the invader. 'Haven't the French and the Germans and the English got their own language? Isn't that how we distinguish them from each other? Then what are we doing with the language of the foreigner imposed on us? We will never be free till we rid ourselves of it.'

Not everyone who loves and speaks Irish does so for political reasons, though a huge revival of Irish speaking coincided with the Troubles period. Republican prisoners learnt it to reinforce their Irish identity and also to enable them to communicate with each other and their visitors without the prison guards understanding them.

Modern republicanism had rediscovered its interest in the old language although few members were native speakers.

Brother Beausang, who ran the Fáinne awards for competence in Irish, bestowed one of those little silver-circle brooches on me when I was thirteen and later told me that he was surprised to find that boys who had been uninterested in the language at school were asking him to come into the prisons and teach it to them there.

Our Fáinne meetings were held on every second Sunday in a dusty old hall with creaky floorboards in Divis Street in Belfast. The first part of each meeting was a speech by Beausang, often asserting the slogan 'Gan teanga, gan tír', 'No language, no country'. We sat and endured that for the sake of the céilí that followed and then we danced with girls from the catholic schools, St Dominic's, St Louise's and Fortwilliam. I didn't know until years later that the same hall was used for IRA swearing-in ceremonies.

Unionists expressed their contempt for Irish and refused to present an Irish language bill at Stormont.

They had read the campaign for Irish as a sectarian concern at the very time that interest in it was being revived by Linda Ervine within protestant communities. Linda was born into a communist family but found christian faith in her thirties and later discovered a love of the Irish language. She had trained as a teacher in her thirties and established classes in Irish language which attracted protestants. Her work with an organisation called Turas – Irish for 'road' – helped undermine the perception that the language was primarily a catholic concern.

Sinn Féin seemed willing to let unionist disdain for the language pass. Some MLAs used a little Irish in the assembly, usually just to introduce remarks to the speaker or ceann comhairle and winding up with 'go raibh maith agat', 'thank you'.

Then one DUP MLA, Gregory Campbell, caused outrage by crudely mimicking the Irish for 'thank you' – 'go raibh maith agat' – with 'curry my yoghurt'.

He followed up with further jokes about Irish vocabulary at his party conference. This was childish stuff but provoked an outraged response when nationalists and republicans might simply have scoffed at a bigot making himself ridiculous.

During the three-year period in which the assembly did not meet there were several attempts to agree a form of legislation that would endorse Irish as an official language, entitling speakers to translations of official documents and to translation facilities if they chose to speak it in law courts. Then some unionists said that if Irish was to be elevated, Ulster Scots should be too.

There was already by then a proliferation of Irish and Ulster Scots in government department names and job advertisements. The Arts Council of Northern Ireland was both Comhairle Ealaíon Thuaisceart Éireann (Irish version) and The Airts Cooncil o Norlin Airlann (Ulster Scots version).

Ulster Scots is a dialect more than a language. Like the Irish language, which had become the language of a peasantry, it has had to be enriched with a new vocabulary. My father would not understand the new words any better than my grandmother would have understood the Irish of the Dublin civil servants.

For instance, in an advertisement for the post of head of the Equality Commission the title was translated into Ulster Scots as 'Eeksy peeksy scheme head yin'.

The Ulster Scots word for a telephone is 'langbletherer', 'lang' being 'long' and 'bletherer' being 'talker'. There are problems with this. The way my father used 'blether' would have been to describe gossip or longwinded, frivolous talk. It was a disparaging word. And that was in the character of Ulster Scots as my father spoke it. Many of its terms were well understood by their native users to be insulting, glib or reductive. It is inconceivable that this dialect could be honed into a fit instrument for practical communication and still be what it was. You can't imagine a woman 'langblethering' home to say she's been delayed at the office.

If my father thought someone was stupid he would say he was a quare gulpin. 'Quare' was an interesting word in that dialect. I always assumed that it was simply an accented use of the word 'queer' but the meaning was completely different. That which was 'quare' was a marvel not an oddity. When you said something was 'queer' you meant that it was unusual and despicable in its oddness. This has been changed by LGBTQI+ culture, which takes the old derisive term and treats it as a routine and acceptable label. When you say something is 'quare' you are speaking highly of it. Usually. A 'quare gulpin' was not an odd or unusual gulpin but an extraordinary gulpin, one so stupid and awkward that you could only think him exceptional, bordering on being a pure lig. Actually, I am not entirely clear whether a lig is more stupid than a gulpin.

A woman was never a gulpin. She might have been a lig.

A pint of stout might be a quare pint. A good boxer might be a quare boxer.

Another example of a word being used to mean its opposite was 'doubt', as in, 'I doubt we'll have a fair bit of rain the day.' Meaning, 'I expect we will have showers today.'

My father had several words denoting quantity but all vague and unspecific so I never learnt whether a wheen was more than a lock or a rake. This way of speaking seemed to me to derive from a rural, lawless culture in which men discussed business in ways which another listening in would not understand. It wasn't exactly code but it was a way of casting a mist over everything said.

And this language was rarely affectionate or positive, though a child or a girl might be addressed as 'cutty'. It was a way of speaking that was always informal and laced with irony. That official documents such as census forms are now translated into a reinvention of this patois is something my father would have scoffed at. I could see him dealing with a trader and saying something like, 'Give us a rake of them yokes', and being understood, then hanging on for a brief natter. 'Did ye year what yon gulpin's up to now? A clatter o weans to raise and he's no more wit than that shower o hallions up the town.'

That's a sample of the dialect I heard at home and which my father carried over from his own childhood in Derry. There isn't much more to it. I doubt there were even a hundred distinct words. It was never something other than plain English to him, with a wee twist to include his peers and baffle his children. It was, essentially, men's talk. I never heard my mother call anyone a gulpin.

This dialect was not much of a vocabulary but more a way of phrasing English.

'Where would you see the likes of that?'

'There's no two ways about it.'

Ulster Scots is freighted with attitude.

Updating it into a serviceable language through inventing new words changes it into something different, misses the point that it was not a medium for formal communication adaptable to the city office or the courtroom. It was the slang of canny countrymen talking out of the sides of their mouths. It was not a written language but it may have been the speech of people who had little formal education. My father left school at fourteen. I never received a letter from him or saw him read a book, though he read the newspapers avidly.

Seamus Heaney called the colloquial speech of the rural people the 'hearth language'.[1] It was the way of speaking that people had picked up at home round the fire from their parents and neighbours when they gathered to talk about the day they had had in the fields or at market.

You cannot formally add to a hearth language. You cannot tell people they used words at home that they didn't and you cannot prescribe new words that they ought to use, because that is entirely at odds with the spirit of what hearth language is.

Some of that language was caustic and discriminatory.

In an Ulster Scots version of the 2001 census form the traveller was called a 'suiler'. This word is a pure invention taken from the Gaelic 'ag siúil', meaning 'walking'. I phoned up Lord Laird, who was head of the Ulster Scots Agency, and said, 'Surely the word your father and mine would have used for a traveller was "tinker"?' And he agreed.

In the most recent census of 2021 that category has been changed to 'Airisch Treveller'. It would be politically incorrect to say 'tinker' but the dialect of my father conceded nothing to such values.

I don't believe that anyone in Northern Ireland will have been able to understand with ease these instructions on the 2021 census form because no one had been exposed to written text like this until this generation.

Heid-coont 20an21:

Whut ye need tae ken

Whut tha heid-coont bis

Tha heid-coont onlie cums aboot yinst iverie 10 yeir an gies us a pictèr o aa tha fowk an hoosehauds in Norlin Airlann.

There is a question about sexual orientation:

Whilk yin o tha follaein gies tha maist siccar accoont
      o yer sex airtin?
Straucht or airtit owerby tha tither sex
Gay or Lesbian
Airtit at baith sexes
Ither sex airtin

The likely hearth tongue terms for gay would have been 'pansy', 'queer' or 'nancy boy'. I don't know what word they would have used for lesbian and wonder if the concept even existed for them.

An alternative to all these answers is: 'Rether no let oan', or, as the same words would be written in English: 'Rather not let on.'

This phrasing has a timorous tone which might indeed be that taken by a self-conscious countryman with something to hide. There is a world of difference between 'not letting on' and, as in the English version, 'preferring not to say'. Not letting on, colloquially, suggests harbouring a guilty secret, or at least implies canniness, an awareness that attitudes to oneself would change if the information was disclosed. This is precisely the kind of implication that those framing a neutral legal form like the census seek to avoid.

That one line shows up the problem of translating the hearth language into formal declarations on legal documents. The language itself has no neutral words or phrases. It is always a vehicle for emotion. It is words and phrases that people resort to for emphasis. This is what makes this census form so funny. I can't help laughing at it but I am not laughing to scoff at country ways of talking. What is funny is the mismatch of colloquial hearth language and the formal legalistic tone.

Seeking to advance the language by giving it statutory recognition in order that legal documents can be translated into it is a whole other project than preserving it. It is effectively constructing a parody of it.

Today Ulster Scots is a unionist cause developed to meet the Gaelic culture with one that protestants could be similarly proud of as proof of their having distinctive cultural roots, but there never was one population speaking Ulster Scots and another speaking Irish. Many champions of an Ulster Scots revival fully understand that, yet like lovers of Gaelic they see their tongue given a political relevance by campaigning parties in opposition to each other.

And they don't protest against this political appropriation of their language interests, presumably because it is generating funding and promotion.

Neither language has exclusive roots within a sectarian identity. A growing number of protestants are learning Irish, though there is little obvious catholic or nationalist interest in Ulster Scots. But the political party which demanded an Irish language act was Sinn Féin. Unionists opposed that and reached a compromise on a language act that similarly promoted the status of Ulster Scots.

The two sides had yet again divided an issue between them to emphasise their distinctness from each other.

Both the Ulster Scots movement and the Irish language movement have made the same mistake of thinking that they can promote their languages by having them adopted – and adapted – by the state for use in legal and formal situations. Because their concerns are for esteem and recognition and parity with each other, this is the measure of recognition, authority and respect that they have chosen. But this approach seeks to change the function of the language rather than to enrich it as it is.

Because they are more concerned with community identity than with language and culture for their own sake, they have campaigned for respect for the languages, according them some parity of status with English, and failed to simply nurture them in their own natural conditions.

The Irish language was modernised by a Dublin civil service to make it fit for official documents such as acts of parliament. The script was romanised in the sixties when I was learning the language at school. The old capital *T* that looked like a *C* with a bar across the top became the ordinary *T* in English. Other letters changed, most notably the *g* which had had a flat top and looked otherwise almost like a 3 with half of it below the line.

The script also lost the sébhiú, or the dot over a letter, substituting it with an *h* after it, as with the *b* in sébhiú, to give it a *v* sound. We retained the fada, the little upstroke to accentuate a vowel, but it tended to disappear from common usage when Irish words were quoted in English. Most newspapers referring to the political party Sinn Féin simply write Sinn Fein.

In recent years editors, particularly English ones, have been more diligently concerned to honour the fada. When I dedicated a book to my friend the poet Ciaran Carson who was a native Irish speaker, my editor asked me to check with him where he wanted his fadas to go. He laughed and said he never bothered with them.

I doubt that a serviceable language for official use could be constructed out of Ulster Scots in the way that one was built on the Irish of my grandmother. That Irish was sneered at by middle-class Dubliners before the war of independence. Ernie O'Malley, who was to become an IRA leader, said that as a boy he was insulted when people addressed him in the Irish form of his name. 'That was not my name. Only the poor used it.'[2]

Now politicians and others will often open a speech with a paragraph or two in Irish to pay homage to the language and assert their identity but will nearly always continue in English, the better to be understood.

In 2020, in the heat of a nurses' strike, Sinn Féin dropped its three-year refusal to return to partnership government. The British and Irish governments had put together a document called *New Decade, New Approach* and called on the parties to agree to it. It would enable the assembly to help the nurses, whose need provided the moral force required for the parties to get back to work. The document also provided for an Identity and Language Act which would create separate commissioners for Irish and Ulster Scots.

This legislation was to be passed in the first mandate of the assembly, that is before May 2022. The DUP refused to co-operate, saying that at a time of pandemic there were more important things to be dealt with. Then a change of leadership in the DUP created the need for a reappointment of ministers and Sinn Féin refused to co-operate unless the language act was guaranteed. The Irish language was still a divisive concern with nationalists and republicans pushing for its promotion and unionists resisting that. To settle the matter the British government intervened and agreed to pass the Act at Westminster. On this particular issue, Sinn Féin seemed unconcerned about British rule.

The *New Decade, New Approach* document had promised to 'respect the freedom of all persons in Northern Ireland to choose, affirm, maintain and develop their national and cultural identity and to celebrate and express that identity in a manner which takes into account the sensitivities of those with different national or cultural identities and respects the rule of law'.

Lord Caine, presenting the legislation to the House of Lords, said, 'It represents a balanced package of measures that ... recognises Northern Ireland's rich diversity of identity and language, and benefits both Irish language speakers and those from the Ulster Scots and Ulster British tradition.'

The good lords hearing this might have assumed that Irish and Ulster Scots were the languages of the common people in Northern Ireland rather than minority cultural interests elevated into crucial elements of contention on which the predominant political factions had chosen to ground their historic dispute.

In fact, the leadership of unionism was not primarily concerned to promote Ulster Scots. It was not an issue that it would have crashed the executive over. Most would have preferred that there was no language act at all.

Sir Jeffrey Donaldson, the leader of the Democratic Unionist Party, had coupled the Irish language concern not with Ulster Scots but with the Northern Ireland Protocol of the Brexit Withdrawal Agreement. He said that passing the language act without dealing with the Protocol would be favouring one community over the other. So, by implication, he had rejected the idea that legislating for Ulster Scots balanced unionist concerns with those of nationalists. Irish language and the Protocol were now fully sectarianised, one being a concern of nationalists, the other of unionists, despite there being no logic to either campaign being exclusively linked to one community. After all, some protestants spoke Irish and some catholic business people had problems with the Protocol.

Linda Ervine, the language rights activist, makes the point that having an Irish language act is a very British thing given that other British minority languages, Welsh and Scots Gaelic, have legal protections.

This argument has not impressed unionists.

And you are still much more likely to hear people in Belfast speaking Polish or Bengali than either Irish or Ulster Scots.

In Belfast many streets have Irish language names. These are almost exclusively in catholic areas. A campaign to allow dual signage similar to that used throughout the Irish Republic resulted in a decision by Belfast City Council to allow streets to have an Irish translation alongside the appointed English language name if 30 per cent of the residents of the street applied for that. In some catholic areas you can see streets with Irish names close beside streets that only have the English form, or original name.

In July 2022 all political parties other than the unionists on Belfast City Council approved a more relaxed system for approving dual signage. By this system, one person in a street could ask for a translation of the name. Then the council would consult with other residents, and if 15 per cent approved, the new signage would be erected.

The logic behind this approach was that the signage should recognise the rights of smaller language groups. It would have been inappropriate, apparently, to follow the wishes of the majority of residents when the whole point was to protect the rights of the minority.

And this right to dual signage to honour a disadvantaged culture is now extended to all language groups, so that Poles and Bengalis and others can now have street signs in their own language if 15 per cent of their neighbours approve.

On 29 July 2022 I was invited onto the *Nolan Show* on BBC Radio Ulster to discuss the new arrangements with former Unionist councillor Chris McGimpsey, SDLP councillor Carl Whyte and stand-in presenter Vinny Hurrell.

Carl Whyte defended the arrangements as consistent with United Nations guidelines on the protection of minorities. Chris McGimpsey said his concern was that 'the way the Irish language has been weaponised will give a sectarian image to Belfast. Prod streets and catholic streets would be identifiable.' This was going to be my main argument too.

Whyte said, 'Let's not fall into the same old language and jargon around this debate. The Irish language has speakers from all backgrounds in Northern Ireland. There are church of Ireland groups. There are presbyterian groups. I know methodists who speak Irish ... Virtually all place names in Belfast come from the Irish language. Most surnames come from the Irish language. This is something that belongs to

us all. There was the Irish language revival in Belfast started
by presbyterians ... It can hardly be seen as a bastion of
nationalism. So we can't go down this road that it is for one
side or the other side.'

I thought he was naive in supposing that Irish street
signage would not be widely regarded as marking an area
as catholic and nationalist. The status of the language had
just recently been the prime contention between Sinn Féin
and the DUP. We'd had three years of a stalled executive
over that single issue.

I said, 'This should have been a decision for the whole
region and not a street by street decision. Carl is being
incredibly naive if he thinks that Irish language street signage
won't simply serve much the same function as flags, painted
kerbstones and murals as identifying streets as belonging to
one side or the other.'

Carl agreed that people in protestant areas like east Belfast
might not want Irish language signage but that they could have
Ulster Scots. 'It is true that people in east Belfast might not
want Irish language street signs but they are entitled under
this policy to get Ulster Scots dual language signage.'

Then Vinny Hurrell asked what would happen if there
were applications for more than two languages, say the Irish
speakers, the Poles and the Bengalis all applied for their street
sign in their own language. After all, there are up to six lots
of 15 per cents in any street so what do you do if more than

one language group gets more than the mandatory 15 per cent support?

I said, 'I speak a little Hindi. I would like to have Devanagari street signs on the Ormeau Road. But I don't think I have an absolute right to have that.'

Whyte said I was being flippant and not taking the language issue seriously, but surely I have as much right to identify as a Hindi speaker as an Irish speaker has, who has also learnt that language in adult life having grown up, like most of us, speaking English.

I said, 'Recognise the key problem in Northern Ireland, which is division, cultural and sectarian division, and stop adding to it.'

11

Mixed Marriage

We heard the band when we stepped out of the car opposite the church, brass and drums on the breeze. My first thought was that this was an Orange band, perhaps a commemoration of some occasion in the protestant calendar that I wasn't aware of. Where I live in Belfast Orange bands in season frequently walk down the main road from the Orange hall at Ballynafeigh.

Then I recognised the tune, 'The Foggy Dew', a sentimental nostalgic dirge in tribute to the Irish volunteers who staged the Easter Rising in Dublin in 1916. A republican band?

Anyway, I had no time to engage with the thought because we were going to a wedding, but it had occurred to me for a moment that maybe some orangemen were making a point about the wedding itself. This was an inadvertent sectarian thought of my own, presuming that protestants were more likely than catholics to be upset by a mixed marriage.

Ross, a young protestant, was marrying Eileen, a catholic school teacher, and it seemed just feasible to me that a few local lodges were annoyed by this, and less feasible that they were celebrating.

As we stepped into the porch of the church, sheltered from the wind and the sound, I asked the man handing me the order of service if a local band had come to enliven the occasion. 'I don't think so,' he said. 'Some anniversary probably.'

Inside people were settling themselves in the pews, meeting friends and neighbours and work colleagues of the couple, the catholics supporting the bride on one side, the protestants supporting the groom on the other. The catholics dipped their fingers in the holy water font as they came in and made the sign of the cross over themselves; they knew to genuflect at the end of the pew before stepping in and sitting down. They might do these things cursorily, hardly noticing that they were doing them. Some would kneel and say a brief prayer before sitting up and chatting in a whisper with a companion for they believed they were entering a sacred space.

Some of the protestant relatives had declined to come in. For them, this was not a church. Their beliefs did not allow for a sense that God was more especially present in one place than in another or that a clergy person had powers to mediate grace and forgiveness. All that stuff was complete nonsense to people who met in small gospel halls and who believed that you formed your own relationship with God through faith or not at all.

That morning demonstrated the different complex layers of Northern Irish sectarianism. For some it really is about theological differences, differences that are actually offensive to them; the idea that you need a priest to connect you to God, that he conducts an essential rite on your behalf and has power in his hands to turn bread and wine into the body and blood of the Lord. For others it is appalling that decent neighbours would regard the pope as the anti-Christ, that they would think that you have your mind controlled by cynical and manipulative clerics.

But it was a lovely wedding. The couple were radiantly delighted to be getting married with their friends and families around them, and you could hardly hear the music.

At communion the catholics went up to receive and filed back to their pews to pray. The protestants on the groom's side of the aisle, supporting Ross, were invited to come up to be blessed, to stand in front of the priest and fold arms across the breast and humbly accept his channelling of God's grace. None did for none believed a blessing from him was of any more value than a handshake.

Ross's aunt and uncle were among those who hadn't come to the wedding.

Ross says, 'They were presbyterians and they wouldn't go into a chapel. Not specifically because it was a mixed marriage but because it was a mass.'

Eileen had asked that the marriage service should not be a mass so that protestants would be more comfortable and not have to be refused communion. 'But the priest said no, no. It has to be a mass,' Eileen recalls. 'Now I still have a wee bit of grit in me because of that. We were forced into that. I didn't feel it was right. I didn't think there had to be a mass.' Nor did there. She knows that now.

There was a catholic priest and a presbyterian minister and they looked relaxed together, though they must both have been aware that one was the host and one was the guest. This was different from what I had expected. My catholic upbringing, under a schooling that started in the fifties, included the assumption that a mixed marriage was a misfortune. The Catholic Church had seriously discouraged it and for most of the twentieth century imposed a law that a catholic needed a dispensation from a bishop to marry a protestant. The bishop would then usually exact a promise that the children of the marriage would be raised as catholics.

We in the church, who were happy about the marriage of Ross and Eileen, felt that we were part of something a little bigger still than the ordinary wonderfulness of two people loving each other and making a commitment. This had social relevance. This was indicative of change, even if it couldn't have been managed with a bit more consideration, even if the chauvinists were out on the road drooling contempt. This was a sign of movement towards the kind of society we wanted.

And the bandsmen outside knew that. That's why they

were drumming and puffing – 'it was better to die 'neath an Irish sky'…

No it wasn't.

We weren't there to celebrate death and honour martyrs. Of course there was the crucifix in front of us and the altar, and the ceremony of the mass and communion which re-enacts the Last Supper and the conversion of bread and wine into the body and blood of Christ. In the Irish republican consciousness the Easter Rising maps readily onto all of that, blood sacrifice, dying for the nation, and even calling it a 'rising' rather than a rebellion ennobles it and connects the idea of a risen people, in catholic imagination, with the resurrection of Jesus.

Eileen says, 'I asked my dad, what's that music? And he said, aw, God knows. Nothing to do with us. They kept it from me.'

She says, 'One thing that I just cannot forgive is that a republican band played outside the church. I didn't know for three years that that band had done that to protest at our wedding because my daddy didn't tell me.'

Ross says that local people visited band members afterwards to rebuke them for what they had done. People came to Ross and Eileen to apologise.

Ross knew. 'I didn't tell Eileen because I knew it would really annoy her.'

And now, angry as she still is, Eileen sees a funny side to it too. 'Ross's aunt, who is really religious, a presbyterian, she gave them money. They had a collection box. She thought, isn't that lovely, the wee band playing for Eileen and Ross.'

But they weren't playing for Eileen and Ross; they were playing against them.

*

There is a lot more mixed marriage in Northern Ireland now than during the Troubles. Then an anthropologist such as Anthony Buckley could theorise that the greatest driver of sectarianism was endogamy, the social sanction against marrying out of your community. Not only did the rule against marrying out consolidate each sectarian community, it also preserved the traditions of ethnic exclusivism for another generation.

Writing in 1995, he said that the importance of the endogamy rule in Northern Ireland could scarcely be overstated. 'It is the rule of endogamy that makes ethnic identity in Ulster an ascribed identity. And while there is some space to negotiate ethnic identity in Ulster, it is the rule of endogamy that makes this space so confined.'[1]

Buckley appears to have been wrong about this, for mixed marriage is much more common now than it was when he was writing, nearly thirty years ago, yet, despite that, sectarian structures remain intact. He taught that sectarian division was a social construct and he accepted that actual cultural distinctions between catholics and protestants were minor. If writing today, he would have to ask what maintains the sectarian structures now when the main driver in his day has lost its force.

In the past, a frustration for journalists writing about mixed marriage was that couples understandably did not want to declare themselves in public. Some had had a petrol bomb through a bedroom window, scurrilous graffiti on a gable wall, their car burnt. In the context of the level of violence at that time, most such incidents would hardly have made a news bulletin but they had the effect of driving couples out of their homes and neighbourhoods, of signalling to the rest of the community that marrying out would be dangerous.

In one horrific case in Ballymoney three little boys were burnt to death. Jason, Mark and Richard Quinn were the children of Chrissie Quinn, a protestant, and James Dillon, a catholic, living on a protestant housing estate. A group of UVF men threw a petrol bomb into their house. This was on 12 July 1998, three months after the Good Friday Agreement, at a time of protests against Orange parades going through catholic areas, particularly through the Garvaghy Road in Portadown. But that was decades ago.

Strangely when I spoke to mixed marriage couples more recently they started out telling me that things were different now, that they had had no problems. And then they started telling me their problems.

Eileen told me, 'It was Mammy said to me, your daddy says you need to finish with that protestant. And I said, well, I'm not going to. And then it was like, O dear, how do we manage this? And then it was kind of forgotten about.'

Her mother hadn't met Ross at that point.

'Once she met Ross she loved him. And she was cross with me when we did break up at one point. But before she knew Ross as a person he was "that protestant". It wasn't that she was sectarian. I think she was scared for me. She didn't want me putting myself in that situation because of where we live.'

Sectarianism is more societal than individual. That's why it counts for little when people try to disclaim their prejudices with 'but some of my best friends are protestants/catholics'. That's irrelevant. It's never about whether you can have a drink with Billy or Seamus, for it's easy to make an exception for the one you get on well with. Sectarianism is the presumption that a community on the other side is different from yours. At the personal level the difference is small, a weak force. Collectively it marks whole communities as distinct, which are either welcoming or closed off against you.

Eileen's mother was being perfectly rational in fearing that her daughter might be exposed to abuse and even danger when travelling to a protestant area to meet her boyfriend. She knew that hundreds of catholics had been murdered by protestant loyalists during the Troubles. The sectarianism of others required that she exercise some sectarian discretion in the protection of her children.

And first impressions of Ross's family were disturbing. His father was an Orangeman who played in a band and marched on the Twelfth of July. When Eileen first visited the house there was a large Union Jack flying from the garage. In England that might be a nice festive thing. In Northern Ireland it is a declaration of allegiance and a marker of territory.

Eileen says, 'Mammy was terrified that I would meet somebody that would take me out of our community and put me in danger because there was a lot of activity around here at the time of the Troubles. The only issues we had back then was the like of that.'

Ross says, 'My dad wasn't in a kick-the-pope band. He had his own views and he believed in them. He was delighted we got married and he loved Eileen. From Day One.'

It wasn't Ross's father's fault that Northern Ireland was riven by sectarian division, even if he was firmly on one side of that divide. He had every right to be an Orangeman and to fly the Union flag from his garage to declare his Britishness. He had no resentment against his neighbours for being catholic. He was perfectly happy to have a catholic daughter-in-law. But he marched on the Twelfth with others who would not have been pleased about that at all. They were his brethren.

Things might have been less complicated if Ross and Eileen had not found each other.

When I sought out mixed marriage couples to interview I remembered the difficulty I had had in the past in persuading people to speak candidly on record about their marriages and their difficulties. My first approach was always to the Northern Ireland Mixed Marriage Association (NIMMA). Today, of course, the term 'mixed marriage' seems dated. Every marriage is mixed. Back then there were no same-sex marriages. There were few migrants living in Northern Ireland, small Indian and jewish communities which perhaps had similar concerns about young people 'marrying out' and seeing their communities and congregations shrinking.

And the discussions about gender identity had hardly begun. For the purposes of this book I am talking about marriages between Northern Irish catholics and protestants, not essentially heterosexual, though the couples I spoke to are heterosexual. I am assuming that a same-sex couple or a mixed race couple would face still greater concerns within their families and the wider society.

The communications officer for NIMMA is Paul McLaughlin, now a grey-haired and wispy man in his late sixties. I didn't need him to find a couple for me to interview. When I cast around I realised that five couples in my immediate friendship circle are mixed. I hadn't even noticed that.

Paul says that he gets fewer people coming to NIMMA to discuss the difficulties in their mixed protestant/catholic marriages than when he started there in 2008. He credits that decline to the marvellous website but says, though no one counts them, that there are many more mixed faith relationships now than back then. He accepts rough estimates that 10 per cent of marriages were mixed or 'inter-faith' when he started in the job and that as many as one in five would be in that category now.

He laughs about the old problem of the BBC coming to him to ask him to put forward couples to be interviewed every time he published a report, for there were mixed marriages inside the BBC and those people weren't coming forward either.

Clearly things have changed in many ways. Society is more secular. Change has been rapid. Many couples don't get married at all and many that do are not religious, but among them some still want to get married in church and they feel a pressure to define themselves according to a single denomination because that may determine what school their children will go to.

Indeed, some just want to get married in a church for the photographs. I know one couple who got married in the City Hall then nipped into an empty church nearby with the photographer, with nobody's permission, to get a picture that would reassure religious relations.

Paul says, 'I actually was humbled from day one in the job when a girl phoned me and started to tell me her problem. This was probably the first opportunity she'd had to speak to someone. And she actually said to me, you are the first person I have told this to. And I felt a lump in my throat. She couldn't tell her parents because her parents were the problem. Her fiancé's parents were slightly less of a problem but still a difficulty. I nearly cried because that person was trusting me with the most confidential part of her life and from then on I have actually been asked, Are you a priest? At which I almost fell off the seat.'

The problems facing these couples ranged from the practical questions of schooling for the children, where to live in a region in which nearly every town and housing estate is definable as protestant or catholic, and how to get on with the relations in a culture which values connections to cousins and aunts and in-laws.

'All you need back home is one bigot in the extended family. If Granny is sitting in the corner and she hates taigs or she hates prods, things are going to be difficult for you. And unfortunately that is more common than we'd like to believe. That screws up Christmas.'

Paul thinks there may be a class element to this too. It is easier to live at peace in a mixed marriage if you can afford a mortgage. The violence tends generally to be in areas of public housing.

In the traditional working-class areas, whether in the older redbrick parallel streets or in the housing estates, extended families tend to cluster together, grown-up children still preferring to settle in streets they are familiar with, often round the corner from Granny who can look after the kids. In that kind of environment the outsider feels more conspicuous. In those communities there are more likely to be paramilitaries. These are organised neighbourhood thugs, professing to be politically motivated, who may run crime in the area from drug dealing to extortion, but they are integrated into those communities too and can provide services like recovering stolen goods, kneecapping other criminals.

To the paramilitaries, the outsider is a threat not just through being from another religious community but also through not having grown up in those streets and learnt the mores of caution and respect.

Frank and Rosie agreed to talk to me. Frank is a boffin of some kind. He works in computers on a level beyond my comprehension and travels for his job. Rosie is a substitute teacher and is available to schools which need temporary staff to cover for sickness, maternity leave, whatever. She has worked in both catholic and state schools, which are essentially protestant.

Frank says, 'It is strange to me that there is such a thing as a mixed marriage association. It's normal to me. There were no voices in my family saying they didn't really like this, none at all.'

Rosie's experience was a little different. 'My mum is a feminist and she only said it the other day how much she cannot have Catholicism.'

Rosie was deeply religious in her childhood and speaks of her pentecostal background as a painful connection that occasionally causes her anxiety about whether she has drifted too far from God. She wanted a religious ceremony for their wedding but not in a church. The compromise was to hold it in a hotel with a liberal-minded methodist minister cheerfully conducting the service.

Then after the wedding, as they started to have children, Rosie found herself moving closer to the Catholic Church, not because Frank wanted her to, but because she wanted to go to church and found the catholic context more genial. She isn't allowed to receive communion in a catholic church but doesn't mind going forward to receive a blessing.

Frank never goes to communion. 'I don't go to mass unless Rosie brings me. Am I a believer? We could talk all night about that. I would be lying if I said I didn't get something out of it. I kind of zone out. It's very similar to doing a meditation.'

He has been to services in protestant churches too.

Eileen and Ross also decided to raise their children as catholics. This was what the Church in past generations would have insisted on yet both couples volunteered for it. Ross, the protestant, says, 'We tried to be sensible. We decided they would be catholics for the simple reason that we were going to be living in a catholic community. It was going to make it easier for them to fit in.'

Eileen was still a church-goer at that time in her life. Ross says, 'I have never been a church person. I used to be. I went to Sunday School and to church every Sunday but I saw so much wrong with the Presbyterian Church when I was younger.

To me it was all about money and who was wearing the nicest hat. To me, that is not being a good christian.'

He had even been a member of the Orange Order as a boy and marched once on the Twelfth.

Frank and Rosie were more likely to find each other than Ross and Eileen were. In a city centre pub in Belfast, young men and women would meet and connect without knowing until they got closer whether they were from the same religious background. In many ways, sectarianism functions like ordinary racism but without the obvious marker of skin colour so connections are easier to make at first.

Eileen says, 'Ironically, I would say we would never have met, only that I went from the catholic school to the high school to do an A level. Doing so, I met a group of girls that I became friendly with and it was one of them that introduced me to Ross. One night I was out and one of the girls said, come on over, there's a boy wants to meet you in the pub across the road. That was the pub the protestants went to. I was in the catholic pub. I swear, you couldn't make it up.

'We went over, and that is how I met Ross.'

Both couples discovered in time that the wider extended families had secrets to guard. Frank had a cousin who had been in the IRA. Ross had a brother in the British army.

Frank assured Rosie that his IRA cousin was regarded as a 'bit of a balloon' in the family, though the IRA regarded him as a hero.

Ross was simply not allowed to tell Eileen about his soldier brother. She lived in an area where many republicans lived and until Ross's family knew her better they were not going to confide information to her that might, through her, even inadvertently, reach some who would be a threat.

Rosie and Frank also encountered that wariness among people in the security services who would keep their distance from a catholic they didn't know.

'We went up to this barbecue with my brother and a lot of his friends were in the police and they would not take Frank under their notice. It was like they had their catholic radar on. It was deeply uncomfortable and I was so ashamed. Now, they weren't my friends. I knew the host, but the taste in my mouth made me feel I would never move back home.'

Both Rosie and Eileen have been school teachers and have worked in schools across the divide and been challenged by pupils from a different background. Eileen says, 'I remember once we were doing a Heaney poem that has some Irish in it and I spoke the Irish and this girl went, "Are you one of them?"

'I said, "What do you mean?" And she apologised. She said, "I just know because catholics are far more crack." Then she asked me if I could speak Irish and I said I knew a bit and they were genuinely interested. And I remember one child said, "And do you believe in it?"

'And I said yes. I don't really go to church but I was thinking, Don't bloody well start coming at me, girl. It was an interesting conversation and it was a safe conversation in a nice room with nice kids.'

Rosie's experience was similar, scrutiny first expressed as suspicion and then turning into curiosity. 'There was a child in a catholic school where I was teaching. And I was teaching about Christina Rossetti and just how puritanical she was, and I was on a rant about puritanical christians, and I finally said, "But not all protestants are like that. Some of us are very normal." And a wee girl went wow! And the jaw dropped and she went, "Are you a protestant?"

'And I said, "Yeah, I am." I swear, her jaw was still down there by the end of the lesson.'

She says she knows one school where a child was discovered to be a protestant and was bullied so much that he had to move class. 'The kids in the class he was moved to were fine with him but there was a clique in the first class that weren't going to accept him.'

I know a story that contrasts with that about a child who came home from a mixed school and told his mother that some of the children there had called him a taig. The mother told me, 'I complained and the head called in the parents of the kids and told them they would be expelled if they did that again. That stopped it.'

While Frank's family is Irish and catholic his parents took care to give their children names that didn't immediately mark them out. They felt they were fortunate to have a surname that didn't brand them either. For many of us, when we introduce ourselves we are immediately identified as belonging to one side or the other. An Irish name like mine says catholic, with nationalism implied. Protestants often do something that catholics don't; they name a child with a surname from the extended family. I know a man whose first name is Johnson, another who is called Wilson.

If you tell me your name is Watson Curry or Morgan Hatfield, I will know you are a protestant. If you are Seamus O'Connor or Soirse Donnelly, you're a catholic.

Frank and Rosie's children are now baptised catholics who have made their first holy communion and go to catholic schools. It worries Rosie's mother, though she attended the baptisms. She had to stay away from the first communions because of covid-19 so they don't know for sure if she would have been happy to go.

Occasionally there are indications that the children are growing up with beliefs that are alien and unattractive to Rosie. When she lost something one of her children said she should pray to St Anthony. That's his delegated role in Heaven, to find things. Rosie explained that as a protestant she didn't do that.

Frank says, 'That's why she can never find anything.'

*

Then there is Tommy and Attracta. Their experience is different because Tommy married a catholic but still identifies strongly as a loyalist. And while Ross and Rosie have essentially settled into a catholic culture, Tommy remains a loyalist and Attracta has put Catholicism behind her.

Tommy grew up in an army family, marched and played with a loyalist band and supports Rangers passionately. Attracta grew up in a catholic family that loved traditional Irish music and she often enjoyed folk sessions in pubs.

The first challenge was reassuring each other that they were safe when they went out together on one's home patch, Tommy particularly being alert to signs up in bars and clubs that identified the space as nationalist or republican. In protestant bars he would often not use her name, calling her T – for 'Tracta.

'It's how he heard my name the first time we met,' she says.

The two traditions came together at their wedding.

Tommy says, 'There were loyalists at the wedding who were involved in stuff. And then just protestants. On Attracta's side we had traditional music played by her family and there were Irish speakers at it, and then my brother was playing the bagpipes. He was in the army. My father was a drum major, and my brother would be interested in the traditional music anyway.'

Tommy was adamant that their children would not go to a catholic school.

Attracta agreed. 'I didn't want them being indoctrinated because I just felt we were so indoctrinated as children, I thought it was damaging. I would have much preferred it if we could have sent them to a school where all religions were taught. So we went for a state school, and then of course, they had their own special version of indoctrination.'

They had to complain about an evangelical group coming into the school and telling children that they could not be united in Heaven with dead relatives if they were not saved.

Tommy would prefer that there was no religion taught in school at all. 'Even the integrated school our boy went to for a time fell back on the religious stuff instead of just scrapping it. In my view, integrated is the way to go and religion should be out of school but they still bring it in.'

Neither is religious now.

Tommy says, 'Growing up I wasn't a church-going boy and then I had that thing that a lot of protestant ones do, I guess, I became a christian for a stage and started going to church, after an acid trip. That was when I thought the world was ending.'

But he questioned everything, even once calling at the minister's house to challenge him on some evident contradiction he had found in scripture.

Attracta stopped going to church at fifteen, to the horror of her mother.

'I challenged her about religion and all of that when I was a teenager and I was astounded by her inability – of this intelligent woman – not to be able to hear what I had to say. I had done religion at A level and it tore apart everything that I understood about the Bible and how it was written. I was so excited. I was thinking, I can't wait to tell Mammy she doesn't have to do any of this shit any more, but it was a brick wall.'

But religion is not the problem.

Both have worked across the divide. Tommy felt uneasy at an event attended by the then Sinn Féin president Gerry Adams and worried about photographs being taken that might show him in the company of republicans.

Attracta has been more relaxed about going into loyalist bars. She says she trusts her friends would not take her to places she would be unsafe.

People do not comment to their faces about their being from different sides, but once Attracta wore a piece of Gaelic patterned jewellery to a club frequented mostly by protestants and learnt afterwards that there had been some discussion about what it might mean.

'It was just a wee Celtic design,' says Attracta. 'I found out later people were wondering what this thing was round my neck. Was I going to cast a spell or be saying prayers over them? Things like that were quite amusing.'

Both say that they retain different ideas about political fundamentals. In the Brexit referendum, Attracta voted Remain, Tommy voted Leave.

He is proudly opinionated. 'There's a lot of things – if they are in the news – I will have strong views on, and I recognise the more things get challenged then the harder your views become on things.'

Attracta says, on the other hand, that the more she is challenged the more she considers the other perspective.

Tommy has been more abrupt at times, more defensive of his position. 'In the early days in particular I would have said things and then realised I shouldn't be saying them. We would have had more opposing views then.'

The one thing that Tommy holds onto as defining him culturally is his support for Glasgow Rangers. He would like to march with the band again but knows he probably won't. He would like to hang out a flag occasionally but he won't do that either. He won't describe himself as protestant unless challenged to defend loyalist politics. But he will not give up on his passion for Rangers.

'Football is a big thing for me. Rangers. I would watch every match. I don't even use the name of the other team. I call them the Septic or the Gypsies. Attracta doesn't get that. For me it is a different thing than the religion. It's a football thing.'

Attracta is confident that everything else in Tommy has 'evolved a bit'. Not this.

He won't give up his love of Rangers and his contempt for Celtic. 'We have an agreement that we'll just leave it. It's very strong for me and it goes back as long as I can remember.'

Attracta accepts that they are different. 'We have different opinions on things and it has taken a long time to reach the point of proper respect for the fact that somebody else has a different point of view, maybe just learning to be open about challenging the stereotypes in your head. There is always that sense of other that is drummed into you in Northern Ireland and it is just trying to open yourself up to finding what's in common rather than what's different.

'I suppose a curiosity about this different culture. It has taken a good while – there's parts of me – we all have this engrained – there would have been a time I felt that a united Ireland was a romantic idea. And probably when I was younger that would have shut me down from understanding what it must be like to be from a different background where that very idea is abhorrent.'

Doesn't being constantly challenged put a strain on a relationship?

Attracta says, 'The relationship has been challenging but always comes good in the end. Because we have come from such different places and had to face into debates which haven't always been easy, it means you start to look at other areas of life, as well.'

The self-questioning that such a marriage imposes on them extends outside the marriage to a wider range of considerations than the questions their differences raise.

'What are my assumptions on this? Should I look at this another way and get a different angle on it? I think it makes for a more rich debate because you do have to challenge your own thinking on a whole lot of different levels.'

But is she challenging her own thinking more than he is his?

'No, honestly, he has come a long way. He was a bit rough when I first got him.'

Mixed marriages are more common now than twenty-five years ago. Some are more of a struggle than others. Maybe the hopeful atmosphere created by the Good Friday Agreement has helped people relax into such relationships and to be optimistic about the future. But the old theory that sectarianism was passed on from generation to generation through the social sanction against marrying across the divide no longer works. Sectarian division is still strong despite these marriages being more readily accepted.

12

Integrated Education

There is a simple answer to the problem of sectarian division, or at least a lot of people think so. And those who are most likely to prescribe it are people who live outside the country and observe violence and the tensions from a distance. You can hear this in calls to phone-in programmes during times of stress and danger. Invariably someone with an English or American accent will say that the obvious cause of division is the segregated education system. Fix that, educate children together and they will grow up without fear and suspicion, and that will put an end to recurring violence.

There is a logic to this, that it might at least ameliorate inter-communal stresses.

The case against integrated education is that it is an indulgence of the middle classes who don't want their children mixing with the boys and girls from the rough areas. Or worse, that it is tearing children away from their roots so that they don't understand their own family backgrounds. It is denying them the cultural heritage which is theirs by right. And catholic priests have said that it is a huge disservice to children baptised catholic to deny them a catholic education which can nurture them in their faith and enhance their prospects of salvation.

There are two school systems in Northern Ireland which dwarf the integrated sector. There is the state system which was established at the founding of Northern Ireland. The intention of the first Northern Ireland government was that this would be a system open to all pupils. Schools which were previously run by Protestant Churches were transferred to this system so there is a strong legacy of protestant religious input.

The catholic schools refused to participate and managed their own system outside direct state control. By this measure they ensured that the state system would be effectively protestant and, their own system being catholic, religiously segregated education would continue within the new state.

I went to school under the catholic system. I started school in Ballycastle, on the north Antrim coast, where I was taught by nuns. I was in the 'Babies' class. This was mixed, with boys and girls together. Sister Marie, a nun in full habit, was our teacher. I recall little of the experience but a few things registered from that time. One was a ruling against little girls coming in wearing trousers. They were told to come to school in skirts. We had no uniform at that age.

Another thing was that we had corporal punishment. We were not caned, however, but slapped on the outstretched palm with a piece of light wood from an orange box.

And one humiliation for me was that I could not drink my school milk through a straw, so I was sent home with a box of straws and instructions for my mother to get me to use them at home until I had mastered the technique. I think the problem was that I was sucking too long on the waxy paper and it was softening and sealing.

And I remember distinctly sitting in class once for a lesson about Jesus and his father and realising that I was totally bewildered and had no idea who they were talking about. The teacher was saying that if you did not love Jesus you would not go to Heaven, so there seemed to be a lot at stake in getting this right.

Religion was important. The nun leading prayers at the start and end of the day would make the sign of the cross over herself backwards, from the right shoulder to the left, so as not to confuse us, providing a mirror image for us of the correct way, from left to right.

We moved from Ballycastle to Belfast when I was five years old so I had to start school all over again. This time, school was the pavilion of the Casement Park Gaelic football pitch. I can still recover the smell of it, the damp concrete and urine, with a smidgen of sawdust.

We went there because the Catholic Church had not yet completed building a school for the new housing estates in west Belfast. At mass on Sundays there was a collection for the school building fund. Our parents were paying to build our school even though they were already paying tax to a government obliged to provide free education.

The new school, the Holy Child, was opened in 1959. One half, for the boys, was dedicated to St Dominic Savio and the other to Maria Goretti. These were exemplars for us, a boy who had tortured himself to purge his sins and a girl who had forgiven the man who raped and stabbed her.

By now the parish was overflowing and additional masses were held each Sunday in the school assembly hall. When I cast my mind back I only remember horrible things. I wince more at the memory of seeing other boys being punished than I do at recalling the occasions when I was beaten myself, always on the hands, always with a cane and 'six of the best' being the most severe you'd expect. I got that once for bad handwriting. And one boy got an awful lot worse, effectively flogged. He had run away from home in an effort to join his father who was in the British army in Germany.

In secondary school I was taught by the Christian Brothers, a celibate order of men mostly from the south of Ireland, and lay teachers employed by them. We had one protestant teacher briefly. She came in to teach us art. Some of the boys taunted her, rattling rosary beads at her.

I had no idea whether this was anything like the experience of protestants in their schools, whether they had prayer, a crucifix on one wall and a statue of the Virgin Mary on another.

In our school, Catholicism was deeply intermingled with Gaelic culture. Prayers were often said in Irish. One value in the separate system is that it preserves Gaelic culture and helps to preserve a coherent catholic Irish community, but that should not be the job of the Catholic Church.

Today catholic schools argue against the need for integration and boast that they have many pupils who are not only protestant but muslim and hindu and from other traditions. The state schools make a similar argument, that there is no need for an integrated sector because their schools are open to all faiths, and always have been.

One of the factors determining the character of the schools is the sectarian division of territory. I might want to send my children to a catholic school for no better reason than that I live in a catholic area, where all their friends are catholic. Sending them to a state, or de facto protestant, school would remove them from their friends and involve the inconvenience of them having to travel further to get there and back.

Similarly, if I had protestant children, I might only want the best for them, that they go to school with their friends and neighbours. And knowing that there are occasionally violent tensions between protestants and catholics, does it not make more sense for children to go to school within their own communities where they will not be accosted by bullies from the other side?

Parents don't want their children to have to walk through protestant streets to school in the uniform of a catholic school. Mercy College is a catholic school serving children from Ardoyne in north Belfast. To save the children having to pass through a protestant area in Ballysillan a local charity, the Flax Trust, provided a bus for them. The Education Authority normally only provides buses for children who have to travel more than three miles to school and this did not apply to the Ardoyne children going to Mercy. Then in 2022 the Flax Trust withdrew funding from the bus service, it only ever having been intended to be temporary.

Coverage of this problem in *The Irish News* raised no questions about whether the children walking to school would be in actual danger. The striking thing about the story is the ease of the assumption that catholic children would not be safe passing through protestant streets. And this may be true.

SDLP councillor Paul McCusker was quoted in the paper saying, 'It is outrageous that parents and pupils have been left in this position so close to the start of the new school year ... I have been working with parents who are understandably at their wits end to resolve the situation.'

The principal of the school, Martin Moreland, wrote to parents advising caution. 'If you have no alternative but to let your child walk, I must urge that you discuss and advise your child on the safest route to and from Mercy.'[1]

That part of north Belfast saw the worst sectarian violence of the Troubles including a protest by loyalists against children going to a catholic primary school, Holy Cross, in 2001 and 2002 when primary school children had to be escorted by police and soldiers. One morning protesters threw a blast bomb and pictures went round the world of small children crouching for safety, screaming in terror.

Segregated education may be a generator of sectarianism but it is also a response to it informed by each side's wariness of the other.

The appeal of integrated education is probably strongest for mixed marriage families averse to having their children raised solely in the tradition of one parent. That was the concern of Kellie Armstrong, the Alliance Party MLA, who is married to a protestant civil servant and has several protestant in-laws. There are strong republican and GAA traditions in her family too. Yet she faced sectarian taunts from a neighbour when going out with a protestant boy.

'I had been going out with a fella from Portaferry and had finished, and then I was going with a fella from Loopland up in Cregagh, and my neighbour says, "What is wrong with you, why are you going with Mr Black when you could have a good fella from down here?"'

The boy wasn't actually called Mr Black. This is a slang term, though a more common variant of it is 'black bastard', a term used to describe a protestant who is thought to be bigoted against catholics.

She says, 'And that sort of sickened me with him. It was a joke with a jag.'

At that time she had an aunt who had become a protestant and two protestant cousins. 'They were in and out of my house all the time. But all of a sudden they were part of that "Mr Black". That was part of my family.'

She served as a councillor for the Alliance Party on Ards and Down Council, which she described as 'a vicious bear pit'. She says, 'They made pig noises at me and you would have had people saying, sit down and shut up, you should be at home looking after your children. You're a disgrace. Anything to undermine you. Particularly from a couple of members of the Ulster Unionist Party at that stage.

'Alliance was a small party and we were seen to be irrelevant.'

In 2016 she was elected to the Stormont assembly. That assembly collapsed within months when Sinn Féin withdrew from partnership government with the DUP, staying out for three years to back a demand for an Irish language act.

When the assembly returned she put forward a private member's bill to require that integrated schooling be the first option considered for any new school established by the Department of Education. Unionists and the Catholic Church opposed this measure. Unionists argued that it would drain resources from the state sector. The Catholic

Church felt the new law would back a rival system against its own.

The bill passed into law in May 2022, just before another assembly election and another collapse, this time with the DUP refusing to appoint ministers or vote for a speaker, protesting against the Northern Ireland Protocol of the Brexit Withdrawal Agreement.

Kellie Armstrong says, 'What annoyed me most was that parents had to set up an integrated school, not government. And if parents wanted to change or transform a school, parents have to drive that too. And in the early days of integrated education it was parents remortgaging their houses to do that, but you don't have to do that for a maintained [catholic] school and you don't have to do it for a controlled [state] school.'

One of the founder parents of an integrated school was the poet Gráinne Tobin. Gráinne and her English husband Andy lived in Annalong, one of the most beautiful parts of Northern Ireland, between the Mourne Mountains and the sea. They had suffered some sectarian abuse there and their home had been attacked.

She says, 'We were a little one storey cottage right on the street, not even a pavement between us and the road. We had done up the place. I had bought every door knob individually and these kids came to the door and said, "Can we put bunting up on your gable?"

'And I said, "We don't really do bunting. Can you not just put it on the next house?"'

This was the wrong response. Gráinne was an experienced teacher and felt she understood teenagers and believed they were usually amenable to reason.

'Andy would have backed down but I didn't realise there was anything to back down about.'

But it wasn't the teenagers she had to worry about, but older, harder men who asserted the Orange character of the village and who were not going to have limits set upon it by catholics moving into the area.

'When the pubs shut this guy came round with a small but dedicated mob. And there were some kids because it was a light summer evening. And this guy threatened Andy with a knife.

'I actually came out and said, How dare you use language like that in front of children.'

The man with the knife was very angry.

'And he had people behind watching him so he couldn't afford to back down. They insisted on putting the bunting up so we had to thole [put up with] having this bunting on our roof so after that we just went away for the Twelfth every year.'

And in later years there were more threats and even windows broken.

She says now that this is something she doesn't like to talk about because it suggests that she had bad neighbours. She also says she felt ashamed at having boarded-up windows after an attack because they advertise to the world that someone thinks ill of you.

First she was part of a project to start a small integrated primary school, though being a busy mother it was Andy who did 'the hard committee work' of getting it established.

'There was huge need, a lot of people had deep personal need for this, like us.'

Gráinne had had experience of teaching inside the state education system and had found it to be more focused on manners and discipline than on learning. She had observed how difficulties that arose between people from different communities were often attributed to those differences. She had once been asked to join a meeting to discuss sex education and then shocked those around her by using the word 'masturbation'. In a sectarian context she feared it was natural for her protestant bosses to regard her ability to talk about sex as being a catholic trait, while she saw their reserve as protestant.

She says, 'I realised I had shifted in their minds to being some kind of dangerous person.

'My friend who was a straight-laced evangelical protestant said, "But they are not spiritual people. It's not that." What they were was deeply respectable, tight-arsed "keep your flowerbeds neat" kind of people.'

Gráinne wanted to be part of building a new education system that would bring children together to develop early understanding of each other without learning the reflex of resorting to stereotypes like these.

'The parents had to create the new primary school for their children themselves. No one else was going to do it. Eventually they got some Portakabins, I was there helping to paint the Portakabins. There were dads there digging the foundations. We were on the site now occupied by a builder's yard in Newcastle, out the back of Supervalu, and it was all DIY.'

They had to pay a taxi to take their child the eight miles to the school from Annalong to Newcastle for want of a school bus.

They were being treated as awkward rebels. The local church kept the children from the integrated school apart from those from the local catholic schools, organising first communion on a different day.

'Sometimes you got remarks which were a bit barbed but which the seven year olds didn't have a clue about but the parents would be bristling, about the importance of keeping kids well battened down in the community.'

The school had a rule that protestants and catholics would attend each other's special occasions so protestant parents baked a cake for the catholic children to celebrate their first communion and a mixed school choir sang at the mass.

'The priest consented to it but in a spirit of making it obvious that this is a bit different, not quite proper. You are there on sufferance and you were made to feel that.'

With children coming through an integrated primary school the parents needed an integrated secondary school for them.

'And we were so lucky to get Kevin Lambe; Jesus we were lucky.'

*

Kevin Lambe, who was raised a catholic on the Falls Road in Belfast, became the first principal of Shimna Integrated College. He tells a story of his initial acquaintance with sectarianism. He was eleven years old. He had just started at big school, St Mary's Christian Brothers Grammar School, on the Glen Road in Belfast, just across the road from the secondary school I was attending at the same time. Kevin is just a couple of years younger than I am.

His sister was going to another catholic grammar school, Dominican College, Fortwilliam, in north Belfast.

Kevin was close to his big sister and happy to oblige when she asked him to go shopping with her. She wanted a new pair of shoes and, as everybody knew, the best shoe shop in Belfast was Reid's in Sandy Row, a protestant area. He accompanied her wearing his school blazer.

'We were walking towards the shop and this guy came along in the opposite direction and just as he passed us he whispered the words, "you fenian c—" at my sister [the coyness about voicing the full word is Kevin's].

'And I was totally shocked and I don't think I had actually heard the c-word much before but I knew. And I hadn't heard the fenian word much either but it didn't take me long to put two and two together.

'I was pretty angry that someone would say this to my sister but it resonated with me. He doesn't know me. He certainly doesn't know my sister and if he did he wouldn't be calling her names like that.'

So a side effect of the effort to protect children by keeping them in segregated schools was that it made them more easily identifiable by school uniform as catholics or protestants.

Sorcha Eastwood, now an Alliance Party MLA, is a catholic but she grew up in Lisburn, outside Belfast, a largely protestant town. She suffered abuse when she went to St Dominic's Grammar School in Belfast and pupils there took her for a protestant because of her accent and middle-class manners. But because she had to take the bus to Lisburn after school she travelled with pupils going home from protestant schools and got further abuse from them because she was wearing the uniform of a catholic school.

She says, 'I was called a fenian, a taig, was spat on. Yet inside school I was a prod. How does that make any sense? There was just constantly sectarian abuse on public transport. That's the way it was.'

But she says she also met 'a lot of really decent fellas' from one school and that she is still in touch with them.

Kevin Lambe's family ran a small shop and a close friend was the man who delivered sweets to them.

'The only protestant that we knew while we lived in this monocultural environment was Jimmy Ennis. He went round in his van and sold wholesale to my daddy. And he was a wonderful guy. He was handsome. He was talented. He was a wonderful artist. I would say, Jimmy, draw me Mickey Mouse and he taught me how to draw Mickey Mouse. And he used to make cine films and he made *The Lambe Family* – it was an art. And he went to all our weddings and so on.'

The friendship was so close that Jimmy was invited to Lambe family weddings, but when his daughter was getting married the parish priest cautioned the Lambes to stay away for the good of their souls. They declined that advice.

Their shop was in Albert Street and was passed by protestant supporters of Linfield Football Club on the way to matches in Windsor Park in the days before the erection of peace line barriers between protestant and catholic areas. One Saturday a group of supporters went into the shop and beat up Kevin's father. A week later, when they came back, his brothers were waiting for them.

He says, 'It would have been fisticuffs. There might have been a hurley stick involved. Which you may or may not think was good but as a child I was satisfied that these bad guys had got dealt with, but it was incomprehensible to me. Why were they picking on my daddy? Why would they call my sister these things?'

Kevin Lambe, as a grammar school boy conscious of sectarianism, devised a plan with other boys to work against it. They started a group called Contact. One of their projects was to form a band which would play in protestant schools.

'It was a sort of sub-Incredible String Band type of thing. We wrote this song and it is so embarrassing to remember. We called ourselves Eternity and the song was called "Eternity" and it seemed to go on for eternity, so it was aptly named. But we went and played it in Methody and we got a good reception.' (Methody is the popular name for Methodist College, a prestigious protestant grammar school in Belfast.)

At that time Kevin's school, St Mary's, had just won a Schools' Cup for Gaelic football and Methody had won a cup for rugby. So Kevin came up with the idea of taking the Gaelic team to play rugby against Methody and inviting their rugby team to come up to St Mary's and play them at Gaelic football.

'And I went in to Brother Murphy, Big John [the school principal]. He was a hard man like, and I said, Sir, I've been talking to the guys and we'd like to do this. What do you think?'

Brother Murphy flatly refused to allow it.

After graduating in Modern Languages at Queen's University Belfast, Kevin took a Postgraduate Certificate in Education. Then protestant students were sent for their teacher training to state schools and catholic students to catholic schools. He went to St Louise's on the Falls Road, not far from where he grew up. This was an all-ability catholic secondary school for girls, though mostly for girls who had failed the 11+ examination which was required for entry into the grammar school system.

After graduation Kevin got a job there and his experience convinced him that all children benefited when the weaker and the stronger were taught together. When he later moved into the new integrated sector he took with him the principle that such schools should bring together children of mixed abilities as well as different religious backgrounds.

The first integrated school, Lagan College, was established in Belfast in 1981. It was set up by a group of parents with the help of a campaigning organisation called All Children Together. Kevin applied for a job there, against the advice of friends and relatives.

'One member of my family said, when the Troubles get worse – and we were in the middle of horrible Troubles – you'll know who your friends are then. As if to say, your new protestant colleagues will turn against you. I couldn't believe that.'

Lagan College was essentially a religious initiative, a christian response, says the school website, to the perception that catholics and protestants were fighting over religion. Kevin Lambe was an atheist.

'I have never thought that this whole thing was about religion. It's got to do with power. It's got to do with land.'

He saw integration as a political measure and he knew that he was taking a risk by getting involved, for in those days he would not have been able to return to the catholic sector having left it for a rival system.

He was interviewed for the job by the principal, Sheila Greenfield. She received him in her office smoking a cheroot and he liked her because she brought the experience of teaching inside an English comprehensive system.

He says, 'I remember the first class I had to take to examination and they were an all-ability French class and I took them through to GCSE. And I consider them the best results I have ever got. Because only one guy got a D, and for him to get a D was an achievement. GCSEs were introduced as an all-ability exam. And the ones who should have got As got As.'

However, Sheila Greenfield didn't stay and Kevin left to take up a job with the Northern Ireland Council for Integrated Education as a development officer. There he generated a boom in integrated education, helping thirteen new schools to get established.

The Department of Education was now legally obliged to fund these schools but was not anticipating the rapid expansion he helped to drive. 'One official said to me, this is not how we do it. And he was quite angry. He says, first of all you do all these polls and surveys and then you do this and maybe ten years later you get a school. And I said, I'm sorry but that is not how we do it. We will have a school here in September and you are obliged to help us.'

In 1994 Kevin applied to become principal of the new Shimna Integrated College in Newcastle, County Down, by the sea, at the foot of the Mourne Mountains.

Gráinne Tobin says of him, 'He is a man whose moral compass is completely unfailing. I have bottomless respect for him and he is dead normal, and his skills from being brought up in a corner shop on the Falls were fantastic as a school principal because you just need to be able to deal with people so easily and a lot of people can't do that.'

Gráinne herself taught English and Media Studies at Shimna for fifteen years, from 1995.

She says, 'Kevin's philosophy was this: when it comes down to it the thing that we have to do with these children is love them. When he said that, I just teared up immediately.

'He was strong but he never had to cut up rough because he is totally convincing as a grown-up. He was never uncouth.'

At Shimna, Kevin Lambe saw that when tensions arose between protestant and catholic children at the school it was usually over football, the catholics supporting Glasgow Celtic, the protestants supporting Glasgow Rangers, and acrimony growing between them as the teams competed. He says it wasn't nasty but 'a wee bit of tension and triumphalism'.

He hatched a plan. He would take ten boys to Scotland, five Rangers supporters and five Celtic supporters, to see their teams in action. But at each game, all ten would support the one side. When Celtic were playing, the Rangers supporters would cheer alongside their catholic friends, and when Rangers were playing the catholic boys would cheer for them too.

'We went to the Celtic game first. Tommy Burns was the manager and he met with us and it was really nice. But I remember our biggest Rangers fan, Stocky, a great wee fella. He was there and Di Canio scored this magnificent goal against Hearts, who are the Edinburgh equivalent of Rangers.

'Ellen McVea, the vice principal, and I were sitting at one end with the kids, and when the goal was scored, I looked down to see how Stocky was doing and there he was, wearing a Celtic scarf and giving the fingers to the Hearts fans.

'And I thought, what the hell have I done? This is not part of the deal here. But that evening he got back to the hotel and he had a shower and he came down to dinner in his Rangers top. And I thought, that is exactly what you want.'

On the second trip, Stocky wasn't so happy at the Rangers game where they lost the chance to win the league a record tenth time.

Gráinne Tobin says, 'I remember it well. Kevin's a big Celtic fan. Did he not tell you that?'

He didn't.

In school he encouraged other people to take assembly because it was important that the kids saw that there were different people with different views. Gráinne took one from an atheist point of view. Another person did his assembly on how he had discovered integration first among the punks.

Kevin says, 'I decided that we wouldn't have prayer. I would have an assembly based around what was happening at the time. The Omagh bomb had happened while we were there. At Easter we had a 1916 anniversary and we had Remembrance.'

He says, 'Some of them may have expressed religious faith if that was what they believed in but what I introduced at the end of every assembly, I'd say, let's reflect or pray. And we would just be silent then for a minute. That became the tradition.'

Kevin ruled that balance between the traditions was important in the school. That meant that children had to identify as protestant or catholic. You can't have a minority in a school which finds it more difficult to speak up.

'For years, if not centuries, Northern Ireland has been cursed by politeness. You probably experience this too. As soon as you are introduced to someone the other person hears the name and thinks "catholic". And while we were growing up that meant, now, I'm going to talk about this, this and this and not this. So we ended up saying nothing about the things that were most deeply felt by that other person, like their religion, what football team they supported, what games they played. Which are important to you as you grow up.

'So I think and hope in a post-conflict society that those are the things you'll talk about because we are different and we want to find out about each other.'

But the integrated sector is diverse too. While Kevin Lambe's understanding of integration is that a school population should be balanced so that there is no shy minority within it, Kellie Armstrong argues that the school should be representative of its community. She is a school governor in Strangford and just a quarter of the pupils are catholic but the proportion of catholics in the surrounding area is around one in ten.

She also has anxieties about the influence of evangelical religious organisations on integrated schools.

'Some of them would be evangelical and that really annoys me. There are Scripture Unions and things within schools. I would love to see more balance but they are targeted quite a lot. Because integrated schools want to be inclusive they will allow some organisations in that I am not necessarily happy with.'

Ironically, having just succeeded in changing the law to prioritise integrated education, essentially requiring those who want segregation to make their case for it, Kellie Armstrong is not optimistic. Much will depend on who is minister of education, and if that office is filled, as at present, by a party which opposed the bill, she believes the new law will be ignored.

13

Sport

The primary purpose of the G.A.A. is the organisation of native pastimes and the promotion of athletic fitness as a means to create a disciplined, self-reliant, national-minded manhood. The overall result is the expression of a people's preference for native ways as opposed to imported ones.

From *The Official Guide of the GAA*

The *Official Guide* of the Gaelic Athletic Association makes plain that the organisation has a purpose beyond staging competitive matches between Irish counties in hurling and football. That purpose is the unification of Ireland. More than that, it is the restoration of a Gaelic Ireland which covers the whole island and establishes a Gaelic character to that nation as the proper homeland of the Irish 'race'.

The language is chauvinistic, sexist and racist. There can be no successful restoration of Gaelic Ireland without the creation of a 'disciplined, self-reliant, national-minded manhood'. This thinking is so dated that one might doubt that it would be written today even by people who cherished those convictions, for they would know that they were at odds with the prevailing liberal culture of western Europe. This sounds more like the eccentric musings of fascists than the authentic expression of even modern republican hopes for a united Ireland.

This is not to say that most people who engage in Gaelic sports do think like this. I'm sure they don't.

The GAA has come under criticism for endorsing republican culture and the usual riposte to that is that it's all just kicking a ball about a field, that the enjoyment of sporting competition has primacy. Whatever the modern lover of Gaelic sports may say in defiance of their stereotyping as closet militants, the founders of the GAA, the authors of the *Official Guide*, had no doubt that the cultivation of Gaelic sports was intrinsic to nation building. That is what it was for. Having fun on a sports field or cheering on your county came second to all that in the minds of the founders.

Children who are inducted into the sports do not engage with these ideas until they are much older and they perhaps reconcile themselves to them much as many church-going protestants live with the Westminster Confession, or as church-going catholics accept papal encyclicals that they don't even read let alone agree with. People do not always believe what the institutions they participate in profess to believe, and the rewards of membership often outweigh the burden of formally subscribing to dated ideas which they are not routinely challenged to defend anyway.

How many presbyterians really believe that the pope is the anti-Christ?

How many monarchists believe in the divine right of kings?

How many catholics believe that the communion wafer is the actual body of Jesus?

I have a friend who is a devout catholic, a member of a lay order, who loves her gay son and assumes that the supposedly infallible determination of Pope Benedict that homosexuality is an 'intrinsic disorder' is not something she has to take seriously.

Like a church or a political party, the GAA has a core membership with a massive support base which must always be cultivated but which is unlikely to consistently adhere to the ideology on which the association was founded.

My own position is that I do not want to be part of a movement whose aims and principles I do not agree with, therefore I do not, for instance, describe myself as a catholic. I am sure there are thousands of people whose background and general world view and sense of personal spirituality is much the same as mine and who *are* content to call themselves catholic. In a similar way, I would not join the GAA or encourage a child to while it promotes the idea of an Irish race whose nation has been corrupted by a foreign (English) culture. Of course, most people in the stands cheering on Kerry or Tyrone in an All-Ireland final, and most of those enjoying a game at parish level, don't think like that and don't deserve to be called racists just because they are enjoying a game, cheering for their county.

What's obvious is that in the GAA county identity is what matters most, not national identity, not race. But some members do think like that and can logically be called more authentic supporters because they do.

I had teachers at school who firmly believed in the principles of the *Official Guide.* In the sixties I went to a secondary school run by the Irish Christian Brothers. No soccer was played in the school. The only sports allowed were Gaelic sports, plus athletics. The long jump and relay racing were not considered foreign. The school encouraged Gaelic football and hurling and produced star players for the county team. In the school yard we played Gaelic handball, a game a bit like squash where the only bat is the palm of the hand and the ball, usually a tennis ball, is hit up against a wall, in our case a brick wall.

Soccer was not merely excluded from the school culture, it was actively frowned on, yet the boys in the classrooms were supporters of English and Scottish football teams and followed their progress avidly. At that time, those who played for the

GAA were forbidden to play 'foreign sports' and our teachers enforced that rule.

In 2001 the GAA removed a rule banning members of the British army and Northern Irish police, the RUC, from the association. This rule had its origins in the perception of those bodies as imperialist, an occupying force. The relaxation of this rule was surely a moderation of the *Official Guide* and its determination to create a 'disciplined ... national-minded manhood'.

The change was a response to the Good Friday Agreement and the reform of the RUC and a new spirit in the country motivated towards reconciliation and peace-building. The IRA was on ceasefire, Sinn Féin had resolved to share power with unionists, catholics were assured of places in the new police service, so it was appropriate that the GAA would seek to be part of the ameliorative trend.

But perhaps there was a clash between the ideals of the leadership and the convictions of players in the clubs. A year later Peadar Heffron, one of the top players for Creggan Kickhams in County Antrim, joined the newly reformed police service, the Police Service of Northern Ireland (PSNI). He was ostracised by his club mates.

He went on to help establish a team inside the PSNI and became its captain, but in 2010 a bomb planted by purist republicans who rejected the peace process ensured that he would never play again. He survived with serious injuries and had to have a leg amputated.

Later, Heffron, in an interview with a former player and noted sports commentator Joe Brolly, spoke of how he had been shunned by his club and how it had not offered any sympathy or support after the attempt to kill him.

He said, 'When I joined [the PSNI] we were promised peace. A new beginning. I thought I'd remain part of my community, a community I loved. I thought I'd play football for Creggan and drink pints in O'Boyle's. That we'd have children and I'd take the underage teams.

'Now I'm in a wheelchair. I live in North Down. It wasn't supposed to happen. It wasn't supposed to happen.

'It's a life. But it's not my life.'[1]

The club responded to Heffron's comments by saying that there was a context to their shunning of him. This context was allegations of state collusion with loyalist paramilitaries in the murder of a GAA member and the fact that nationalist and republican political parties had not yet endorsed the reformed police service. This suggested that the club took its lead from political parties.

One member said that they did not reach out to him after the attack because that would have seemed hypocritical. An appearance of moral consistency was apparently more important than basic humanity towards a former player.

*

The greatest attraction of the GAA is the sport itself. The teams were organised at parish level. The local foundation of the team is important, establishing a relationship between community and team that is lacking in most major sports. You don't have to come from Manchester to play for Manchester United but an Antrim hurler will be from the county.

The organisation is avowedly non-sectarian on principle, although the organic link to parishes persists and inevitably the organisation is predominantly catholic. Many clubs take their name from the parish in which they were formed, which is usually a saint's name.

The GAA sports ground nearest to where I grew up is Casement Park, named after Sir Roger Casement. He is viewed in the Irish nationalist tradition as a hero. He tried to import guns into Ireland for the Easter Rising in 1916. In British tradition he was a traitor, hanged for his betrayal of his country. The arms that he brought in were imported from Germany at a time when Britain and Germany were at war with each other.

Some clubs honour more recent republican dead, like the Kevin Lynch Hurling Club in Dungiven which is named after one of the hunger strikers who died in the Maze Prison in 1981 in a protest demanding political prisoner status for republican paramilitaries.

The GAA has extended its popularity far beyond a core republican base whose primary concern is the unification of Ireland and the cultivation of a 'disciplined, self-reliant, national-minded manhood' and what is 'good and distinctive in our race', but sectarian attitudes are attributed to the association by critics.

In 2022 some loyalists protested against proposals for a GAA ground in east Belfast at Victoria Park. The ardent loyalist blogger and media commentator Jamie Bryson tweeted: 'The GAA should disavow IRA terrorism & remove from their official guide the purely political "basic aim", instead adopting a neutral political stance. Until then, how could the organisation ever be acceptable to any self respecting unionist?'[2]

The Irish News reported that the GAA in east Belfast had attracted cross-community support but that work on the Victoria Park pitch had been halted because of loyalist criticism.

Nationalist and republican politicians defended the GAA. SDLP councillor Séamas de Faoite was quoted in the paper as saying, 'The GAA ... offer a positive vision of athletic co-operation across east Belfast for the benefit of everyone. It's time for those stuck in the past to get out of the way.'[3]

But clearly the GAA is stuck in the past too when it is declaring officially that the purpose of its existence is the creation of a 'disciplined ... national-minded manhood' committed to the people having control of the 'impaired' national territory.

Sinn Féin's North Belfast MP John Finucane, a former Antrim Gaelic footballer, said, 'There should be no place in society for discrimination against children and young people because of their choice of sport.'[4] But that was to miss the point of the protest which focused on the *Official Guide*.

Journalist Cahair O'Kane wrote an article for *The Irish News* challenging Jamie Bryson's criticisms of the GAA. He listed several members of the GAA who had been killed by loyalist paramilitaries or members of the security forces. 'It's one thing for him [Bryson] having a distaste for the GAA. It's another thing to create tension around the use of playing pitches in east Belfast for Gaelic games.'[5]

He accepts that Gaelic games are mostly played by 'nationalists' and that 'in its early days the GAA and the republican movement were very much interlinked'. However, 'by the time the Troubles came around, they operated as very different strands of nationalism rather than through each other.'

So he is not saying that the GAA is an apolitical sporting organisation without a commitment to a united Ireland, but he compares the GAA's nationalism to the flying of Union flags over some soccer pitches and the playing of the British national anthem at games. 'There are young protestants engaging with the games right across the North. What is it they engage with? It's kicking a ball around a field. That's all it is.'

He argues that scars in nationalism are too deep for centuries of baggage to be dropped, yet efforts are being made to leave it behind. He blames unionism for failing to respond to those efforts.

He says he has never heard any political discussion in GAA team changing rooms.

There is no declared cultural or political affinity in the branding of other sports bodies in Ireland but a sectarian attitude is inferred from the support bases and team profiles of some soccer teams. Linfield Football Club is predominantly protestant but has signed catholics, the first unawares. In the late eighties, manager Roy Coyle signed Tony Coly and caused unease in the team when they learnt that he was a catholic, or had been.

Coyle was quoted in *Sunday Life* in May 2020 saying:

'There was nothing written in the club's constitution about signing Catholics and I was never told not to sign a Catholic, but the club had that stigma at the time and perhaps Catholics from certain areas might have been wary of signing for Linfield.

'After Tony signed, the club went on to sign many Catholics and the two that stand out for me are Pat Fenlon and Dessie Gorman, but it all started with Tony Coly.

'We also signed Abdelli Kammal, or Sam Kammal as we called him, after the piano player in the film Casablanca, where he was from.'[6]

Rugby prides itself on having stayed out of the sectarian rivalry, though in the North it is played mostly by protestants.

Former international Trevor Ringland played for Ulster and for Ireland, and when he played for Ireland he was charging up the field alongside men he had previously smashed into in provincial games.

The nearest thing we have to an embodiment of a Northern Ireland identity is the Green and White Army of the Northern Ireland football team. There have been difficult times when sectarian chanting on the terraces was an embarrassment that drove some of the support base away. It has also lost the team the prospect of signing good players who have preferred to go south and play for the Irish Republic.

But Ringland, who was a member of the Sports Council, cites the changes that were made for the national side as evidence of good work against sectarianism.

'The atmosphere was horrendous, deeply sectarian, unfamily-friendly and the crowds had dropped to five or six thousand for a World Cup qualifier. You could see that the team was uncomfortable being out on the pitch to the extent that I said I would not go back.'

But he could also see that if he walked away from the team it would fall entirely to the bigots. In time, a community relations officer was appointed to work with the fans and get them to see the damage their sectarianism was doing to the game.

'They looked at themselves and they said, what are we like? And they thought, well actually we are pretty horrible. We're alienating people from the game. We're destroying the thing we love so we need to change, and they sought ideas and constructive criticism from critical friends from all backgrounds and new songs. The red, white and blue from the terraces went to a sea of green, the green and white army.'

And when sectarian chanting started up from the terraces they drowned it out with loudhailers or band music. This worked because it was in the self-interest of the club to cultivate the greater support base that was available if they could draw people from both communities.

'You hear stories now that if they are on a tour somewhere and some of the fans start singing the old songs, the old guys go up to them and say, son, we don't do that any more. And the family friendly atmosphere is back.'

But the work to purge sectarianism continues. In September 2022 one of the Northern Ireland national team's star players, Kyle Lafferty, fell for a stunt by a Celtic fan, asking for a selfie. Lafferty stood beside him, smiled obligingly and the Celtic fan said, 'Up the Celts.'

Lafferty's response on a TikTok video isn't so clear that I'd confidently quote it but by general agreement he spat out sectarian contempt for the joker who'd snared him. When that went out on social media he was dropped from the team in advance of a game against Kosovo which, incidentally, they won 2–1.

Another player's offensive tweet from his teenage years appeared on social media then and he was dropped too.

And in October 2022 the Irish Women's national football team took the shine off their World Cup qualifying game in Glasgow against Scotland by singing 'Celtic Symphony' in their changing room. This is the song that had cost boxer Michael Conlan support. It includes the chant 'Ooh Ah Up the 'Ra', 'the 'Ra' being the IRA.

The team had to apologise and the player who had uploaded a video of the chanting onto Twitter was said to be appalled and in tears. She hadn't even had the sense to protect her team mates from the consequences of their behaviour, so she must have had little or no sense that there was anything about singing that song that disgraced them. This became a major news story, with families of IRA victims outraged that past terrorism was being endorsed by women too young to remember the horrors inflicted.

Others defended the women singing a song which was part of a wide repertoire of football songs in the republican tradition. But that argument amounts to a defence of the right of separate communities to have their separate histories and traditions and distinctly different appraisals of the IRA.

It is a defence of sectarianism: you do things your way, we do them ours.

14

Crossover

Though social evolution through intermarriage erodes sectarianism, it does not defeat it. Integrated education develops relationships and cross-community understanding, but it does not break the sectarian mould. Taking sectarianism right out of sport would help, with people on both sides supporting teams and even types of sport they currently see as alien.

The biggest possible and most radical change that is conceivable, to fix Northern Ireland, would be political parties extending their reach beyond their core native communities. Very little of that is happening.

The most intractable expression of sectarianism is the division of territory, but even that might yield, or at least matter less, if political parties could canvass and win votes in areas currently inaccessible to them and in which they have expressed little interest.

When a Sinn Féin candidate can get votes in a protestant housing estate and a unionist can find support on the Falls Road it will not matter that those areas are homogeneous when judged by the religious backgrounds of those who live there.

The linkage of political parties to sectarian community blocs is bad for them. They need to change and outgrow those blocs. Indeed, a time will come, and may already have arrived, when unionism and nationalism have garnered as many sectarian votes as they are going to get and have to reach beyond their native communities to win converts – protestants who will vote for the SDLP or Sinn Féin, catholics who will vote for a unionist party.

Neither side is making much of a plausible effort to cross over and to sell its case to the other side.

When John Wilson Foster published a collection of essays, *The Idea of the Union,* first in 1995 then revised and republished in 2021, he started with a lament that the cause of the Union was being failed by huge sections of society which should have an interest in it but don't. Basically, catholics should see that the Union is good and should vote for it. But why should they rise to a cause that does not inspire them? Surely the failure is in the cause itself or in the presentation of it.

He says that he compiled the book in part because of 'the widespread feeling of many in Northern Ireland that their wish to remain citizens of the UK was not being clearly and forcefully articulated'.[1]

Many people have no wish to upend the Union and they affirm that in opinion polls. The Union is their normality, part of the backdrop to life which is taken for granted but they are not ideologically passionate about it. They don't feel inspired to follow a unionist party. Perhaps many of them don't vote at all because they don't see any party which articulates either their contentment with things as they are or their vision of how things should change.

Foster knows there are people who do not vote for unionist parties but tell pollsters that they are happy to settle for the Union. He wants them to declare themselves. But in the sectarian context of Northern Ireland such a declaration can be too easily read as apostasy, as alignment with unionist traditions bound up with Protestantism, reverence for the monarchy, pride in the imperial tradition. Foster himself seems unable to conceive of a unionism that does not include these things, but the catholic who would vote against a united Ireland is unlikely to be happy with that package of ideas. This is probably also as true of many English people who like the structure of the UK too.

John Wilson Foster does like those ideas and therefore, even in his invitation to closet 'small u' unionists to declare themselves, he alienates them.

His argument for the Union includes strong anti-sectarian sentiments and he criticises unionists 'who have been derelict in the matter of trying to bond with Catholics in a Union for all'. But how well is he doing himself at bonding with those catholics who are content with the Union?

He quotes me as evidence that some catholics might be accommodating themselves to Northern Ireland's position within the United Kingdom. I had coined the term 'provisional unionists'. He liked my ironic pun, echoing the Provisional IRA. Then noted that I had failed to account for those catholics who might be 'contented full citizens of the UK', whatever that means. I pay my taxes and vote in elections and drive on the left. What more does he want from me before he'll regard me as a 'full citizen of the UK'? Who has created this category of the less than full citizen?

In essence, he was suggesting that being resigned to the Union isn't enough. He wants us to really commit. He admits that there is little evidence of catholics wanting to be as enthusiastically British as himself by his standard and blames that on an 'unspoken taboo', not crediting those people with having convictions as valid as his own.

He writes, 'The concept [of catholics wanting to be enthusiastically British] is inadmissible and the word most assuredly is, "unionism" being synonymous with historical anti-Catholicism and anti-Irishness. So the political position of someone of a nationalist background contented with living in the UK cannot be identified and named.'[2]

He wonders if it is also something imposed on catholics by 'muscular republicanism'.

And since he criticises unionist parties also for failing to bond with catholics in a 'union for all' he is essentially identifying sectarianism as the problem. There is almost no exchange of ideas between the two communities. They do not win converts from each other. And Foster has himself failed to win catholics over to his own project.

He published essays from twenty-one contributors and most of them are protestant. How do I know?

We have a little custom in Northern Ireland which anthropologists call 'telling'. This refers to the ways in which we can signal to others whether we are protestant or catholic, or the ways in which we can pick up signals that are perhaps not even consciously sent. The easiest way to sound out someone's religious background here, without putting that question directly, is to ask which school they went to.

In the details of contributors to John Wilson Foster's book, the school the writer went to is named in two thirds of the cases, and other 'telling' signals are included in several biographical notes which don't name the school. This is not usual. I have often had to write a biographical note to accompany an article or a paper, or details for a festival programme. I have never been asked to name the school I went to.

You would think that a collection of essays on a new way of defining unionism would have taken care to diversify its contributors, and this editor's inability to do that undermines his whole case for it proves that unionism is still protestant.

One of the likely reasons that de facto unionists in the catholic community do not declare themselves, or attach the word 'unionist' to their aspirations, is that unionism itself appears broadly content to be protestant and grounded in a protestant culture that is reinforced by a protestant education system and reverential of a protestant monarchy.

Foster observed that fact himself but made no effort to challenge it.

In addition to reinforcing this perspective in a book which declares itself opposed to such thinking, John Wilson Foster is also guilty of conflating all expressions of nationalist sentiment in Ireland together into one broad sectarian front opposed to the Union.

This is a 'them and us' analysis.

The Republic of Ireland, he writes, 'was founded in profound hostility to [the] monarchy and has maintained ever since a low-level version of that hostility, which the recent Brexit negotiations revealed. This campaign had been waged in one form or another since the island of Ireland was partitioned in 1920–21 in order to prevent an all-island civil war but was renewed as an armed insurgency in the 1940s and 1950s and most seriously in the late 1960s which lasted until 1998 with a seventeenth-month [sic] ceasefire from autumn 1994.'[3]

This is the perspective of someone who regards the Irish government of today as continuous with the IRA campaigns of three separate generations and who sees Ireland's handling of Brexit negotiations, in order to preserve its open border, as an extension of the IRA campaign.

This echoes the sectarian prejudice which says 'they are all the same, you can't trust any of them'.

Foster fails to see any distinction between Sinn Féin and the ministers in other Irish parties whose chief political goal at the time of writing is to curtail Sinn Féin.

As for a catholic country being averse to a protestant monarchy, that would not normally be seen as unusual. Ireland, however, has seemed sometimes to be as besotted by the monarchy as many of the British themselves.

He is fixated on the idea that Irish identity is predicated on hostility to unionism and sees the Irish unease with Brexit as an extension of historic anti-Britishness. So, at the same time as proclaiming the right to a British identity he seeks to undermine as invalid any claim to an Irish identity. He says modern Ireland preserves the 'Story' of centuries of struggle. 'Brexit has been a convenient pretext for an oblique re-telling of the Story by the Dublin commentariat.'[4]

A 'pretext'? The Irish apparently had no real problems arising from Brexit but saw it only as an opportunity to be a nuisance to the old enemy, the British, but Foster has seen through that.

And the modern Irish shift towards secular liberal politics and culture are indeed 'radical changes' but they have 'not seriously altered or enlarged the Story'.

He says, 'Mine is the British Story, and the Irish Story, as it is written, won't accommodate it.'[5]

I deal with this at length here to illustrate that a unionist intellectual seeking to reach out to and invite non-unionists to commit to the Union fails lamentably to empathise.

On the other side of the argument, those who call themselves civic nationalists in the Ireland's Future movement have been organising conferences and panel discussions in which they invite unionists to join them in planning for a united Ireland. This misses the point that unionists don't want a united Ireland. Any discussion on the future with them would have to start with an understanding that the Ireland of the future might not be a single polity but some other arrangement.

So, we are seeing the beginnings of efforts to uncouple the core ideologies from their sectarian roots but so far they are naive and fruitless.

Foster's book is a pitch for unionism to be enlarged through Irish-identifying people giving up their understanding of their history and identity. He is essentially setting out the parameters of the sectarian dividing line and insisting that he will not cross it but that others must. And some others have.

*

In the 2022 assembly election the Ulster Unionist Party fielded a rare catholic candidate, Stephen McCarthy. After the Green Party lost its seat in Stormont, a protestant councillor for the party, Simon Lee, defected to the SDLP, a party, mostly of catholics, committed to a 'new Ireland'.

These were small steps towards non-sectarian politics but both the Ulster Unionists and the SDLP were glad of their new converts diluting the embarrassing sectarian character of their parties.

Stephen McCarthy is an eloquent critic of sectarianism. 'We have learnt little beyond pitifully reducing the risk of our sectarianism into an annual tit for tat slabber match,' he has tweeted. 'We have squandered our peace.'[6]

This was in the middle of August 2022 when several events illustrated the nature and degree of sectarian acrimony between two communities. At that time of year, from July to late August, sectarian celebration becomes public and exultant.

The Apprentice Boys of Derry had staged their annual march around the city's walls. This had been peaceful but a street trader was spotted selling flags of the Ulster Volunteer Force and the Parachute Regiment. The UVF is a protestant paramilitary organisation which murdered catholics during the Troubles, often grotesquely, with victims being first tortured with knives.

The Parachute Regiment flag in Derry has a specific reference. It was there that in 1972 Paratroopers murdered fourteen civil rights protesters on Bloody Sunday. The flag has been flown from lamp posts in protestant areas to express support for a soldier faced with prosecution for his alleged part in that massacre.

This coincided with the end of Féile an Phobail or the West Belfast Festival. Thousands of young people had gathered in the Falls Park for a concert at which the Wolfe Tones led chanting of 'Ooh Ah Up the 'Ra', part of the chorus from their song 'Celtic Symphony'.

A rap trio called Kneecap had unveiled a mural depicting a police Land Rover in flames, as if it had just been petrol bombed.

There was more. In Derry a bonfire was erected with wreaths of poppies decked on it as a calculated insult to British remembrance of the war dead.

What appalled McCarthy was that otherwise sensible people rushed to defend the outrageous behaviour of bigots in their own communities, as if defending community cohesion was more important than agreeing with the other side that some on your own side were behaving like savages.

He tweeted, 'Infuriating that every time something like this happens, sensible principled people, decide to engage in a bitter barter, giving special dispensation to "their own", making excuses, finding a recent example of when "themuns" did worse. It's pathetic.'[7]

This is an interesting line. Bigotry, by this analysis, is sustained by 'sensible, principled people', not just by ignorant louts. And they do it through 'whataboutery'. This is a term everyone in Northern Ireland knows. It is the device by which every criticism of people on your own side, even those you don't wholly agree with, is deflated by a counterattack on the other; yeah, but what about Bloody Sunday? What about the Abercorn Bomb?

McCarthy directly criticised Sinn Féin's deputy leader Michelle O'Neill, who had said in an interview that the IRA had had no alternative to its campaign.

He wrote, 'These are the lies sociopaths tell themselves to sustain their delusion.'[8]

Others had connected O'Neill's endorsement of the IRA campaign with the chanting in the Falls Park. What space was there to criticise kids cheering the IRA when the woman in line to be the next first minister said the IRA had had no choice but to kill and bomb for Ireland?

Then a week later LucidTalk online polling found that 70 per cent of nationalists agree with Michelle O'Neill that there had been no alternative to the IRA campaign. This presents a daunting picture of sectarian cohesion.

Or maybe some read her words in different ways. The objective of the IRA had been to create a united Ireland. This simply wasn't attainable by any approach when the IRA campaign started.

Michelle O'Neill probably thinks it is attainable now through political campaigning.

McCarthy was now challenging the republican tradition in more vigorous language than their rivals in the nationalist community, the SDLP, would use. Calling them sociopaths denies any credit to the idea that they were well intentioned, driven by political motivation, though that is how they are understood in the Good Friday Agreement.

But how does he feel about having crossed a sectarian boundary and identified himself with a tradition that previously excluded catholics? There have been some catholic members, notably Sir John Gorman, who served as deputy speaker of the Northern Ireland Assembly from 1998 to 2002. But he was different in that he had a background in the officer class of the British army, not in working-class Belfast. He had served in the Irish Guards during the Second World War and taken part in the Normandy landings. He had worked with the British intelligence services.

Further back, in the sixties, another catholic, Louis Boyle, chair of Queen's University Belfast Conservative & Unionist Association, resigned from the party claiming that his attempt to secure nomination as an Ulster Unionist candidate in South Down was blocked by the Orange Order.

Stephen says his membership and advancement within the party have never been opposed on the grounds of his being a catholic. 'At almost every stage of my journey into Ulster unionism, I have pushed against open doors, receiving an inquisitive welcome, and bewilderment when I speak of expecting anything other than that.'

The only hindrance he says he felt was the expectation cultivated within his own family that unionism simply 'will never like catholics. Will never treat us as equals. Will never accept us.'

He believes he has proven that to be simply untrue.

Stephen grew up 'all over the place', living in both protestant and catholic areas, in Antrim while his mother trained as a nurse, then on the Lenadoon estate in west Belfast where his father's family is from. Later he lived with his mother on the Falls Road and from there they moved to Finaghy and then to a protestant part of north Belfast.

He had started school at the same primary school I went to thirty years earlier, the Holy Child in Andersonstown.

He says, 'From the age of three to nine my mum and I were on our own. She was a nurse, so we didn't have a difficult life, but equally, she very often did without so that I could have a happy childhood.'

In the mid-nineties, while they were in north Belfast, loyalists organised protests across Northern Ireland in support of Orange Order demands for the right to parade through the catholic Garvaghy Road in Portadown and other areas which they regarded as traditional routes, but along which opposition was raised against them.

'Mum got a rap at the door and was advised that they knew who we were, knew I went to Holy Cross [a catholic primary school] and wanted to let her know that she was welcome to stay. They knew she worked in the community but that the street was being barricaded and that it might be best to go and get some groceries. She politely thanked them for the kind advice and after closing the door got straight on the phone to her friend and asked for her help to move out. We were out before teatime.'

From there they moved to Divis and then to Short Strand, both catholic areas.

That was where his mother remarried. Stephen's stepfather was from a mixed background, his mother a protestant from the loyalist Tiger's Bay area, his father from Dublin.

The family moved to the Antrim coast but Stephen came back to Belfast for university and says he still feels like a 'westie', slang for people from catholic west Belfast.

He completed a degree in journalism at the University of Ulster and was invited to apply his communication skills towards helping Ulster Unionist Danny Kinahan with his election campaign and after getting him elected was offered a job as his communications manager.

He took other work with the party and then was selected for a council seat but lost it and would have emigrated, disillusioned with political prospects, but for the covid-19 pandemic. Then the new party leader, Doug Beattie, hired him as a constituency manager and stood him as an assembly candidate in South Belfast, the constituency I live in. He didn't get the seat. He wasn't my first choice but he was on my list. Every voter can vote for all of the candidates in numerical order.

Stephen had previously considered joining the SDLP,

got an application form and then didn't return it. 'I simply gravitated towards the SDLP as they were the party my family supported for generations and because of their social democratic politics.'

He says, 'I am a social democrat. I am proudly left-wing. If I lived in Great Britain I would be an active member of Labour.'

What he couldn't accept in the SDLP was its long-term goal of a united Ireland. 'I simply don't believe it is the right path for Northern Ireland. Although I do appreciate that the SDLP have a more pragmatic, devolutionist approach to it than Sinn Féin.'

Then he joined the Alliance Party.

'However, the greater my political awareness became, the more I questioned Alliance attitudes to the parties around it, in the centre-ground of Northern Ireland politics. I quickly became disillusioned with their obvious hostility towards both the SDLP and UUP, their fellow "centrist" parties, the parties that I always viewed as being the key to Northern Ireland's future.'

He didn't like the Alliance Party's presumption that it could opt out of constitutional politics 'because they feel they are above it'.

He says, 'For me, this leaves people behind, exacerbates division, creates an intellectual hierarchy in our politics, and sectarianises those with constitutional aspirations. It harms community relations and exacerbates division, rather than mitigating it. It stinks of snobbery.'

He rejects the idea that you can turn your back on division in society and damn as sectarian those who take sides on the constitutional question.

He chose to take sides in favour of the Union. 'My unionism is more drawn from the idea that working-class people in Belfast, Glasgow, Manchester, Liverpool, etc. all share many of the same issues, history, traditions and values. Perhaps that's outdated, but I still feel an affinity for it.'

He wants Northern Ireland to work. He says that even if you want a united Ireland you should want Northern Ireland 'oven-ready' for unification.

But unionism is more than a pragmatic reading of what's best for the region; it is an almost exclusively protestant culture with reverence for the monarchy and the imperial tradition. Surely a catholic 'westie' has difficulty adapting to that, given the vastly different cultural background he has come from and feels at home in.

It is well understood that catholics in Northern Ireland are likely not to want to toast the monarch. In the past there had been protests at Queen's University Belfast against students being required to stand for the British anthem on graduation day. This routine has been scrapped in deference to the sensitivities of students who do not identify as British or as monarchists.

Once, I was invited by the then secretary of state for Northern Ireland, Sir Patrick Mayhew, to dine at Hillsborough Castle with a small party of media people. At the start, Sir Patrick said that normally before dinner they would toast the queen but with regard to the sensitivities of catholics present they would waive that tradition.

Stephen says he sees the monarchy 'as one of the last unifying "myths" of the UK and one of the few that most people can agree upon. Therefore, even the leftie in me believes the monarchy is a net benefit to the United Kingdom, and to unionism.'

He was at a garden party at Buckingham Palace and felt 'immensely proud'. He called his mother from a party on the terrace at the Palace of Westminster when working for Ulster Unionist Danny Kinahan to say, 'Did you think when we were riding up the Falls in a black taxi to the Holy Child that I would one day be calling you from here?'

And he has a reading of the imperial tradition that both criticises it and reinforces his unionism. This, I think, is truly novel thinking from a unionist.

'For those people, particularly in England, that look at Northern Ireland as a burden or problem that they'd happily cast adrift, my pro-Union, pro-British sentiments take on a very rebellious hue. Do not invade, plant, nation-build and maintain a presence somewhere if you don't want to deal with the consequences. You don't just get to walk away from Northern Ireland. We are your problem to deal with as much as we are our own.'

He says he hasn't a strong religious faith but retains the values his mother taught him, to treat others the way you want to be treated yourself. 'I had a mum telling me at home that two wrongs do not make a right … treat others the way you want to be treated. At the same time I was hearing older members of my family complain of the injustices of discrimination in their generation from unionism and the protestant community, as though this conferred upon catholics a sense of victimhood that made us always right and all of our actions justified. A sort of arrogant virtue of victimhood. But when I looked at this in practice, all I could see was the same toxic behaviour from fellow catholics towards protestants that we had complained about.'

Another politician who crossed over is Simon Lee. Like Stephen, he passed through other political parties before making a decision to join the SDLP, the Social Democratic and Labour Party which aspires to uniting Ireland.

Simon was born into an east Belfast working-class family in 1979 and studied Divinity at Queen's University Belfast hoping to become a presbyterian minister. He gave up on that idea because the Church was too conservative. He had liberal values of his own which were not shared by the Church so he trained to be a teacher instead.

Now in his forties he teaches philosophy of religion in the A level department at Belfast Metropolitan College to students of diverse backgrounds. He is also studying for a degree in Psychological Trauma Studies. This course is sponsored by

WAVE, an organisation which helps victims of the Troubles. The incidence of Post-Traumatic Stress Disorder is high, reckoned to be the highest recorded rate in the world, though presumably there are trouble zones in which it has not been as carefully studied.

As a young man he was 'unionist by default'. He had turned to the Church because it was what he had known. 'Like a lot of people I had lived a very segregated life. Studying A levels at "the tech" was my first time mixing properly and studying with catholics,' apart from a short time in his childhood when his family moved to Canada and quickly back again.

He was fifteen at the time of the 1994 IRA ceasefire and he was, like most of us, getting a political education through following the unfolding of the peace process, when the daily news was covering intense political negotiations, reporting the IRA's return to bombing, the election of a Labour government in Britain, the resumption of a ceasefire and talks and the developments towards the Good Friday Agreement.

It was a tense and exciting time to be engaged with Northern Irish politics and it felt like an historical phase that would condition our thinking for a generation.

Simon says he struggled with the clause that paramilitary prisoners belonging to organisations which endorsed the agreement would be granted early release, but in the end he was relieved that people voted yes to the package by a substantial majority.

'My journey away from being a unionist to my current thinking around the intriguing prospect of a new Ireland was gradual and complex. I think living abroad had an impact. I spent a year in Chicago in 2000–01 and did a lot of reflection on my identity and our history. My American friends couldn't get their heads around why I identified as "British" while being from the island of Ireland.'

Now, he says, a denial of Irishness does not make sense to him. Scottish, Welsh and English people identify themselves by the country of their birth but Ulster unionists tend not to.

I'm not sure this is a very good argument for constitutional change. Under the terms of the Good Friday Agreement he can freely identify as Irish, even have an Irish passport, and still endorse Northern Ireland's membership of the United Kingdom.

But there was more. 'The social conservatism of much of unionism is and was a massive turn-off. It's frankly embarrassing.'

Much of unionism identifies strongly with the evangelical christian tradition which abhors liberal social values. It resisted the legalisation of homosexuality in the seventies and, more recently, same-sex marriage and abortion.

Both Stephen and Simon have been influenced by Brexit. Both believe it was the wrong decision. Stephen believes that one of the guarantees of the Union was that non-unionists in Northern Ireland were averse to instability. They might not be passionate about the Union but they would prefer to live with it than risk a massive political, social and potentially violent upheaval.

'However, the instability surrounding the Brexit vote and subsequent negotiations has lowered the threshold nationalism needs to reach to influence public perception on Northern Ireland's future.'

The instability is there anyway, so nationalists are able to argue that this is the time to press on for major constitutional change, a united Ireland.

'This is further compounded by a political culture in Westminster that looks unstable and unsavoury, undermining another central plank of the idealist unionist defence – that Northern Ireland needs to be more like the rest of the UK.'

He reads all that as a challenge to defend the Union, not an invitation to usurp it.

Simon sees the same circumstances and reaches a different conclusion.

'By the time Brexit happened I had long left my unionist identity behind, but there is no doubt this solidified my position. It exposed the democratic deficit that somehow goes unnoticed. For example, it struck me that if every voter in NI had voted to remain in the EU, and English voters voted as they did, Brexit still would have happened. The destiny of Northern Ireland was ultimately determined by English voters. This does not feel right.'

And the idea of a new Ireland, united and reconciled, is, for him, a more inspiring vision than keeping what we have.

But can there be a reconciled Ireland?

Not without the total surrender of the nationalist cause, according to John Wilson Foster, and he has some logic on his side. Nations have their narrative and the Irish narrative is of the plucky little country that preserved its identity and shook off the yoke of British imperialism before India and Kenya and the others, and even inspired them to go the same way.

The three major political parties in the Irish Republic continue to celebrate the revolutionary period and trace their roots back to it. We saw this in the 2016 commemoration of the Easter Rising and the 2022 commemoration of the death of General Michael Collins who led the IRA then signed a treaty with the British accepting partition.

A country that defines itself by revolution against Britain cannot comfortably absorb northern territory inhabited by British people who resent that revolution. One or the other has to change the narrative by which it justifies its sense of national identity.

But before merging the two parts of the island of Ireland into a new Ireland, surely there has to be some merger of the two communities. Surely the peace lines have to come down before the border is removed. This is the SDLP's vision of reconciliation, but how is it to be fulfilled?

Simon says, 'I don't think there is anything fundamentally incompatible between being a protestant and aspiring for a new Ireland. However, I'm not up for any form of nationalism that isn't based on a fundamental commitment to human rights and religious and cultural equality.'

Religious sectarianism is not a problem for him. It is rapidly waning.

He thinks the job of bringing the two communities closer together is made easier by the decline of the influence of the Catholic Church. 'Although for historical reasons unionists and nationalists do still tend to break down on catholic/protestant grounds, there are signs that this is evolving.'

And he made his own shift away from stern conservative evangelical Protestantism while still a student.

One of the signs of change in the alignment of political movements with religious traditions is that he and Stephen McCarthy have both joined parties in which nearly all other members are of the other tradition. More importantly, they both say they feel at home in those parties.

I wonder about Stephen attending Unionist Party meetings where there is a portrait of the monarch on the wall or a picture of former party leaders who were candidly sectarian, and whose whole political vision was of a protestant Northern Ireland which they presumed to call Ulster.

Simon, who once wanted to be a presbyterian minister and now teaches philosophy of religion, can perhaps feel more at ease at an SDLP meeting or conference but aren't there bound to be occasions when the humour of his colleagues jars with his own conditioning? Perhaps not.

He says, 'For me the exciting thing about a new Ireland is that it's not merely rubbing out a border on a map. Not merely augmenting Northern Ireland into the existing southern state. It's about something new. In that context the symbols of the new Ireland cannot be predetermined, and that by definition means the flag and anthem have to be part of that important conversation.'

Change like that might be hard for many SDLP members and voters to accept.

The other evidence of some weakening of the towering ideologies and the emergence of a less polarised approach to politics is the growth of the Alliance Party, which refuses to designate as nationalist or unionist.

Alliance was formed in the early seventies at roughly the same time as the SDLP and the Democratic Unionist Party, primarily to provide a forum and field of action for people who felt they could set the constitutional question aside at the time of greatest violence and political deadlock.

It was long derided as a party of trite, middle-class people who had missed the point that politics here is about the constitution before it is about anything else.

Its growth in recent years can probably be credited to disillusionment with the outworking of the Good Friday

Agreement and to the charisma and eloquence of its current leader, Naomi Long.

A generation has grown up since the agreement and found that it has not dispelled sectarianism. That generation, like Stephen McCarthy, believes that the peace has been squandered. The peace lines are still up. Sinn Féin and the DUP, instead of forming a creative partnership, have struggled constantly with each other.

They seemed to be co-operating well when the first ministers were the old bellowing bigot Ian Paisley and the IRA leader Martin McGuinness, but both were brought down by their parties for presenting an image to the world of being too friendly with each other.

Paisley was usurped by his former deputy, Peter Robinson.

McGuinness served alongside Robinson and his successor, Arlene Foster. He and Foster were expected not to work well together but soon the jokers were calling them Marlene, as if they were a single unit. And that was progress in the minds of many; that was the vision of the agreement made tangible.

McGuinness met Queen Elizabeth and appeared charmed by her. The republican base disliked that. And the Sinn Féin share of the vote in 2015 had slipped. The immediate cause of the breakdown of that partnership was Arlene Foster's refusal to meet a Sinn Féin demand that she step down temporarily to allow the investigation into the incompetently framed scheme that was vastly overfunding a renewable heating project.

But behind all this, the republican base was calling McGuinness back to communal politics. He resigned, brought down the assembly, and the party refused to restore partnership government until unionists agreed to an Irish language act. Politics was pointedly communal again and both Sinn Féin and the DUP benefited from that in electoral support.

That's the horrible irony. A sectarian appeal wins votes.

15

The Fix

The first task in fixing Northern Ireland is to diagnose the problem.

In my view that problem is sectarian division which permeates the whole of society. I have shown how it divides people not just by religious background but by territory, language, educational segregation, sport, media, music, humour and political party affiliation.

Twenty-five years ago both parts of Ireland agreed on a solution, the Good Friday Agreement. The agreement was grounded on the assumption that the core conflict was a legitimate political dispute over sovereignty. The agreement and the peace process around it presumed that reasonable people had inherited an historic problem of unresolved sovereignty and it devised a creative compromise to enable all those people to live in harmony and to provide functioning devolved government for Northern Ireland.

The agreement provided for a referendum on Irish unity at some time in the future when a majority for it seemed likely, with Britain committing to letting Northern Ireland go. The Irish republic agreed to relax its claim to northern territory until such time as a referendum on unity had passed. This might have provided a way for political parties to set their constitutional concerns aside, leaving it to the people of the future to decide on a united Ireland and to get on, in the meantime, with building relationships and running the place.

Then ideally, when a referendum was called, people would vote pragmatically for what they saw as being in their best interest rather than by affinity to an ethnic bloc represented by sectarian political parties. Working together would have softened and ultimately dissolved those sectarian loyalties and attitudes.

It was a vain hope. Parties continue to define themselves by their sovereignty concerns and to garner votes from distinct sectarian communities. Many think the unionist support for Brexit, whether admitted or not, was an effort to reinforce the Irish border. Sinn Féin now campaigns for advancement towards a united Ireland, needling unionists by exaggerating its immediate likelihood. Now we should realise that even in a united Ireland the sectarian division would continue and that it would be better dealt with first, before a border poll. Otherwise the border poll will exacerbate division, fire up anxieties and generate chaos.

There was acknowledgement in the Good Friday Agreement that sectarian division was a problem, but it saw this as a symptom or by-product of the sovereignty dispute. Parties were given responsibilities in the agreement to address social division but they did nothing to resolve it. As Duncan Morrow puts it, they accepted the agreement as the ceiling of their achievement rather than as the baseline from which to build a more integrated society.

Morrow says that after the St Andrews Agreement, which modified the Good Friday Agreement in 2006, when the executive was restored after one of its long breakdowns, the British government pushed for a comprehensive policy to try to address sectarianism. The big parties rejected it. The one thing they agreed on most readily was that they should do nothing about the division because they could play on it for votes.

'From the Sinn Féin point of view it was a significant deviation from their analysis that all the problems lay with the British, and from the DUP's point of view, dumping it alleviated them of the burden of acknowledging the problems of religious exclusivism.'

There have been moments since then when parties which benefit by sectarian division resolved to create a shared future, but never sincerely. Duncan Morrow says, 'It was in their joint interest to prove that no movement on either of those barriers was required and that a peace process could be done without dropping any of your fundamental anti-Britishness or your anti-Catholicism. I have just always thought that that was implausible.'

The parties set 2023 as the year by which all of the peace lines would be dismantled. There has been no work on that at all. The Berlin Wall endured for twenty-eight years. The original Belfast peace line has stood for fifty-three years so far.

The 2021 census was welcomed as an indication that Northern Ireland was changing. There are now slightly more people of catholic than protestant extraction, which suggests that neither can now dominate the other. And since we now have a substantial middle ground, largely represented by the Alliance Party, this blocks both republicans and unionists from getting a majority. Logically that should guarantee fairer treatment for everybody.

It also shows that both the big protestant and catholic blocs have to win converts across the divide to expand further. And while it also brings a united Ireland in prospect, making the Union dependent on catholic support, which will be less ideological and more pragmatic, it also provides for a Northern Ireland in which catholics may be comfortably at home here as previous generations were not.

So far there is little sign of the big blocks canvassing for support beyond their sectarian communities. Instead they may be seeking further growth by appealing to non-voters in those communities. And they do this, on the republican side, by presenting a united Ireland as an imminent prospect and, on the unionist side, by raising alarm about the security of the Union.

And even if the sectarian forces are compromised by the new reality, the sectarian social, cultural and territorial infrastructure remains. There is still the social sanction, now exercised through social media, that inhibits people from expressing views inconsistent with the core ideology of the community they grew up in.

It is good that mixed marriages are more common, a quarter of all marriages by some estimates. It is good that the Department of Education is now under a legal obligation to develop the integrated education sector. And there have been some indicators of generosity, such as the Sinn Féin deputy leader attending the funeral of Queen Elizabeth.

It is a hopeful sign that political activists like Stephen McCarthy and Simon Lee build their aspirations and decide their loyalties by individual right rather than community affiliation, and there are others too.

This is not to say that many members of the SDLP, Sinn Féin, the DUP and the Ulster Unionist Party aren't also people of integrity and intelligence. Of course they are, but they must surely be aware that belonging to a party in which every other member was baptised in one church and educated in one system reflects their own failure to sell their ideas. It is a hindrance to growth and in any other democratic society would be an embarrassment.

So how do we fix this?

Sinn Féin would say we fix it by uniting Ireland. Then unionists, like the protestants who stayed in the Free State after partition, will adapt to the new reality and even discover that they have more power and influence in a small country's parliament than they have in the UK.

I don't believe that. I think that the protestant community, or a large part of it, would continue to be a problem if brought into a united Ireland to which it had not reconciled itself.

The SDLP thinks that the approach is to have a new Ireland, built on reconciliation, achieved first. That makes sense except that reconciliation is likely to be a slow process while the prospect of a border poll may arise long before it is achieved. And those who want a united Ireland may get their 50 per cent plus one votes without having won over many people outside the catholic community.

We would then still be stuck with a sectarian society under a different jurisdiction.

The Ulster Unionist Party's solution is to persuade people of the benefits of the Union. But Brexit has damaged confidence in the Union, as has the apparently shoddy quality of the British government in recent years.

The Democratic Unionist Party wants to preserve the Union. Its main difference from the UUP is that it seems much less inclined to extend its reach into a catholic community and defines itself by conservative social morality policies.

Then there is the Alliance Party, which seeks simply to set the sovereignty question aside and is criticised by both the SDLP and the UUP for failing to build a more solid middle ground by criticising them for retaining their identity-based ideologies.

Someday a decision will be put before the people of Northern Ireland on whether they want a united Ireland and, on present form, many will vote simply according to how a reading of their birth certificates would predict.

The emergence of a middle ground creates the necessity for all parties to compete for votes there. That may have a moderating effect. If Sinn Féin and the DUP want to colonise the voter base of the Alliance Party then they will have to frame policies that appeal to people who are sick of sectarianism and the sovereignty question.

One thinker close to the heart of the Alliance Party said to me, 'To date, just about the only thing [nationalists] seem to agree on is that the work – and the risks – to build support for and deliver Irish unity should be undertaken by everyone else except northern nationalists.'

He added, 'Nationalists are so convinced that the Republic will vote for unity that they devote almost no time to the possibility that support could turn against them when the full implications of unity come into focus during a campaign.'

He pointed out that northern nationalism has lagged consistently behind modern Ireland on major issues such as abortion and marriage equality, and that this suggests it is out of touch with mainstream Irish opinion.

Northern nationalists, essentially, form an ethnic group that may ultimately be as resistant to merging with the South as it was with northern unionists. 'Mainstream Ireland may just well decide that its tax revenue is best spent on more important things than quarrelsome money-grubbing Northerners.'

For now the priority should be to restructure the assembly. As prescribed in the Good Friday Agreement, there can be no government in Northern Ireland without cross-community power sharing. That has enabled large parties, Sinn Féin and the DUP to pull down the executive simply by walking out, even when they have held less than a third of the seats. Power sharing was established to incorporate the nationalist minority. With the balancing of the two factions the same protections are now needed by unionists. Neither side trusts the other to govern.

Labour and the Conservatives in Britain don't trust each other either, but they accept that they must allow each other into power if that's what the electorate determines. We have yet to progress to that base line of acceptable acrimony by which politics functions in other democratic countries. We should aspire to it.

Yet for the middle ground to grow, it has to find ways of not alienating people who cherish their identities as nationalist or unionist. That seems to be a harder task. We have to reach a point at which it is perfectly all right to espouse nationalist or unionist views without being assumed to be representing a sectarian faction. The only way this can come about is through those ideas winning converts across the divide and becoming uncoupled from ethnic identities. People should argue for the Union or for Irish unity on the basis of reason and evidence rather than as an expression of ethnic affinity.

Racist and sectarian insults have to be removed from the discussion. That requires us to criticise those from our own camp who are offensive in promotion of their factional ideology. It also requires us to allow others to cross over, in either direction, as Simon Lee and Stephen McCarthy did, and not to bombard them on social media with charges that they are turncoats or rebels.

So what might imaginative interference in this sectarian balance seek to achieve?

It would pull down the peace walls, preferably with consent and support for the communities divided by them but ultimately within a clear time frame and regardless of what people say they want. The peace walls affect more than just the streets butting onto them; they symbolise and consolidate division across the whole of society.

They set limits to the extension of social housing, not just protecting sectarian communities but preserving them.

The marking of territory with flags, murals and graffiti will have to be stopped. Where flags are hung from lamp posts the police should simply take them down.

Some will argue that the Union flag and the Irish tricolour are legitimate expressions of sovereign identification, the Good Friday Agreement allowing us all to identify as British or Irish by birthright as we please. The agreement says nothing about how whole streets or lamp posts may identify themselves.

The murals which celebrate paramilitary organisations or distinguish an area as predominantly catholic or protestant should also be removed. Most of them are on gable walls of properties rented from the state anyway. Some people will be very touchy about this and object, and will probably object more strongly still if any move is made to remove the memorials to the dead that have been illegally erected and tolerated for years.

Where these memorials honour the 'fallen heroes' of paramilitary organisations they should be dismantled. Perhaps a generation has to pass before that becomes possible, but getting rid of them should be a clear objective of those who want to end sectarianism. You can't expect people to be comfortable in a street where there is a memorial to a terrorist who would have killed them and may indeed have killed some they knew and loved.

We would be better off with a single, more comprehensive memorial to the dead of the Troubles or a Troubles museum, but nothing should be allowed to mark territory as home to one side and alien to the other. Proposals for dual language street signage that will ultimately define residential areas by ethnicity should be scrapped. Street signs across the whole of Northern Ireland should have a consistent pattern. Either they should only be in English or they should have three languages, English, Irish and Ulster Scots. Otherwise they become territorial markers of protestant and catholic areas.

Currently there are competing narratives about the past by which factions justify violence and division and obstruct re-evaluation of our experience, a prerequisite to reconciliation. A comprehensive museum of the Troubles, representing all the factions, would enable our children and their children to understand what we experienced while also being presented with the positions and experiences of other factions and the state.

Let them see images of explosions and shootings, the kneecappings of teenagers, the torture in interrogation centres, the young bombers who blew themselves up, the part-time soldiers shot dead on their farms, the religious leaders who whipped up passions, the back alley assassinations, the police officers shot dead on duty, the cynical politicians and the starving hunger strikers and the filthy walls of their dirty protest cells, the agents and informers and their handlers.

Let everything be visible and questionable and nothing actually endorsed as noble or singular or unrelated to everything else. And let this be the only memorial.

A creative and radical response to sectarianism would challenge the Churches to get out of education. The Catholic

Church presumes that nearly everyone who goes to a catholic school and was baptised a catholic wants to go on being a catholic. This hugely inflates the number of people who are actually believing catholics and denies the massive tendency towards secularism. We can see this in the disparity between the many who go to catholic schools, and the few who go to church.

Dispassionate intervention would make an audit of the real scale of the catholic faithful who need a catholic education and would fund that and direct other resources into integrated education.

It is not the job of the Christian Churches to preserve ethnic homogeneity or Gaelic culture. And, while the territorial division endured, we would probably need bussing to get children to schools.

Sectarian chanting and abuse can be undermined with better education. Football clubs are conscious of the problem. Unfortunately, for some, it serves their business model well to appeal to a sectarian faction, yet the Northern Ireland national football team discovered that the opposite approach worked for them. We have seen how boxer Michael Conlan lost support through appealing to one community by marching to the ring with 'Celtic Symphony' playing and how the Irish Women's football team brought controversy and disgrace on themselves by chanting the same song after a match victory.

Their experience should teach them that the larger fan base is attainable to those who are not sectarian.

But songs have power and maybe we need some new ones.

The GAA has made extensive gestures to reform and be inclusive. It has to go further. It should abandon the sexist, patriotic and borderline fascistic language of the *Official Guide* and it should ban the naming of clubs after convicted criminals and terrorists.

On languages it should be understood that Irish and Ulster Scots are regarded as symbols of community identity. Proponents of both should be facilitated to extend their reach into other communities. They would probably be happy with that. It would be in their interest.

The editors of print newspapers need to adopt a responsibility to reach beyond sectarian markets and to do so by demonstrating knowledge of and empathy with the concerns of communities they have tended to ignore. How they do this could be monitored and reported on by a commission.

And part of the fix must be economic. It makes no sense to split the market. A house for sale in a predominantly protestant area is likely only to attract offers from other protestants. You won't sell to protestants if there are Irish tricolours hanging from lamp posts on your street. Sectarianism reduces your appeal to more than half the population. That's why companies are quick to sack employees who show up on social media platforms chanting sectarian slogans; they are bad for business.

The social rift in Northern Ireland is like a family quarrel. These peoples are not alien to each other but they have chosen different paths and neither path is liked or understood by the side that has gone the other way.

This is not comparable to ordinary racism which lights on disparities in wealth and culture, tastes in food, dress and language, even in customs regarding hygiene and sanitation. We don't hear catholics or protestants complain any more that the other is 'taking our jobs', the sort of jibe that is levelled by racists at migrants. Neither openly regards the other as migrant, yet insulting comments that regard protestants as 'planters' and 'huns' are common on social media. The imputation there is that they come from elsewhere, if only from a land twenty miles away and four hundred years ago. But no political leader or politically motivated popular commentator will use those terms. A popular slogan among republicans was 'Brits Out'. Protestants said they felt included in that while republicans defended it as simply an attack on British rule. The stock abusive words for catholics carry no suggestion of them not belonging but they sneer at the Gaelic culture (taig), impute rebellion (fenian) or displaced loyalty (papist).

In political life or in debates on religion, rather than emphasise the fact of division, both sides contend on issues. Yet it is almost as if they agree to disagree for the purpose of masking their fundamental inability to coalesce into a coherent and contented society. They were brought to agreement in order to end violent conflict that had lasted decades, through a peace process, and then instead of putting division behind them they institutionalised it and made peace processing the whole of politics.

In short, everyone needs to know clearly what the problem is. It is sectarianism. It is a blight on this society, contrasting it starkly with political, social, cultural and political mores in the rest of Britain and Ireland. Ending it is desirable. It will be better for everybody.

As it stands, sectarianism is something we should be ashamed of. And it is. Routinely in my exploration of this issue I met people who bridled at the very suggestion that they were sectarian. It is not a word they like to be labelled with. That's understandable.

But if they don't like it, they should do something about it.

Notes

3. The Hate

1 Jamie Bryson, @JamieBrysonCPNI, Twitter, 3 June 2022, https://twitter.com/JamieBrysonCPNI/status/1532625863849693186

2 Moore Holmes, @mooreholmes24, Twitter, 3 June 2022, https://twitter.com/mooreholmes24/status/1532736785029206016

3 Ibid., https://twitter.com/mooreholmes24/status/1532646793015701504

4 Keith Duggan, 'North's united response to vile video perhaps one small reason for hope', *The Irish Times*, 3 June 2022.

4. What's God Got to Do with It?

1 Dr Órfhlaith Campbell, @drorfh, Twitter, 9 September 2022, https://twitter.com/drorfh/status/1568138011065319425

2 The News Room, 'DUP founder: I'm bewildered that Protestant church leaders would welcome Pope NI visit', *News Letter*, 4 May 2018.

5. Who Isn't Sectarian?

1 Jenny McCartney, 'Seamus Heaney's poems are for Protestants too', *The Spectator*, 7 September 2013.

2 Ibid.

3 Patrick Shea, *Voices and the Sound of Drums*, p. 179.

4 Ibid.

7. Race

1 Timothy Kearney, 'Beyond the Planter and the Gael: Interview with John Hewitt and John Montague on Northern Poetry and the Troubles', *The Crane Bag*, Vol. 4. No. 2, 1980/81, pp. 85–92.
2 Seamus Heaney, 'The Other Side', from *Wintering Out*, Faber & Faber, 1972.

8. Stick with Your Own

1 James Kelly, *The Irish News*, 2 October 1999.
2 Brian Feeney, 'There will never be "normal politics" here because the north is an artificial construct', *The Irish News*, 20 April 2022.
3 Susan McKay, 'Queen Elizabeth's death is an earthquake for Northern Irish unionists', *The Irish Times*, 8 September 2022.
4 Kathy Sheridan, 'Queen Elizabeth was the anti-celebrity with global star power', *The Irish Times*, 8 September 2022.

9. The Catholic Paper and the Protestant Paper

1 'Belfast boxer Michael Conlan's pride in his nationality "rubs some people up the wrong way"', *The Irish News*, 12 March 2022.
2 Andy Watters, '"I'll destroy Leigh Wood..." Michael Conlan declares war as tension boils over in Nottingham', *The Irish News*, 12 March 2022.
3 David Kelly, 'Michael Conlan opens up on how he is driven on by pain of past injustice as he prepares for world title battle with Leigh Wood', *Belfast Telegraph*, 11 March 2022.
4 Steve Beacom, 'Jim Boyce calls on politicians to silence match "morons" after Cliftonville and Coleraine reported to IFA over sectarian chanting', *Belfast Telegraph*, 17 March 2022.

10. Languages

1 Dennis O'Driscoll, *Stepping Stones: Interviews with Seamus Heaney*, p. 129.
2 Ernie O'Malley, *On Another Man's Wound*, p. 5.

11. Mixed Marriage

1 Anthony D. Buckley and Mary C. Kenney, *Negotiating Identity: Rhetoric, Metaphor, and Social Drama in Northern Ireland*, p. 6.

12. Integrated Education

1 John Breslin, 'Safety fears for Catholic pupils facing walk through loyalist area to get to school', *The Irish News*, 27 August 2022.

13. Sport

1 Joe Brolly, 'Spurned, bombed and maimed by his own kind', *Independent.ie*, 29 October 2017.

2 Jamie Bryson, @JamieBrysonCPNI, Twitter, 5 August 2022, https://twitter.com/JamieBrysonCPNI/status/1555452407093526528

3 Connla Young, 'Loyalist Jamie Bryson claims GAA not welcome in unionist and loyalist areas', *The Irish News*, 5 August 2022.

4 Statement on Sinn Féin website, 4 August 2022, https://www.sinnfein.ie/contents/64103

5 Cahair O'Kane, 'Kicking Out: Change starts with the man in the mirror', *The Irish News*, 9 August 2022.

6 Stephen Looney, '"My best signing": Roy Coyle recalls Tony Coly's arrival as Linfield's first Catholic signing', *Sunday Life*, 7 May 2020.

14. Crossover

1 John Wilson Foster, *The Idea of the Union*, Introduction, p. 12.

2 Ibid., p. 39.

3 Ibid., p. 11.

4 Ibid., p. 82.

5 Ibid., p. 83.

6 Stephen McCarthy, @smccarthynire, Twitter, 15 August 2022, https://twitter.com/smccarthynire/status/1559276305669029892

7 Ibid., 14 August 2022, https://twitter.com/smccarthynire/status/1558814348461604864

8 Stephen McCarthy, @smccarthynire, Twitter, 4 August 2022, https://twitter.com/smccarthynire/status/1555123563773968390.

Bibliography

Buckley, Anthony D. and Kenney, Mary C., *Negotiating Identity: Rhetoric, Metaphor, and Social Drama in Northern Ireland* (Washington DC: Smithsonian Institution Press, 1995)

Foster, John Wilson and Smith, William Beattie (eds), *The Idea of the Union: Great Britain and Northern Ireland – Realities and Challenges* (Vancouver: Belcouver Press, 2021)

Gaelic Athletic Association, *The Official Guide of the GAA* (Dublin: Central Council of the Association, 2019)

Mitchell, Claire, *The Ghost Limb: Alternative Protestants and the Spirit of 1798* (Belfast: Beyond the Pale Books, 2022)

Naqvi, Saeed, *Being the Other: The Muslim in India* (New Delhi: Aleph, 2016)

O'Driscoll, Dennis, *Stepping Stones: Interviews with Seamus Heaney* (London: Faber and Faber, 2008)

O'Malley, Ernie, *On Another Man's Wound* (London: Rich & Cowan, 1936)

Shea, Patrick, *Voices and the Sound of Drums: An Irish Autobiography* (Belfast: Blackstaff Press, 1981)

Acknowledgements

A great many people helped me with this book. Some of the interviewees have preferred to be given pseudonyms or to be anonymous and I have obliged them in this. Special thanks go to Kellie Armstrong, Sorcha Eastwood, Claire Hanna, Kevin Lambe, Simon Lee, Stephen McCarthy, Seamus McFadden, Paul McLaughlin, Claire Mitchell, Duncan Morrow, Matthew O'Toole, Frankie Quinn, Trevor Ringland, Wallace Thompson and Grainne Tobin. My thanks to James Nightingale at Atlantic Books and my life-saving editor Tamsin Shelton. Also to my agent Lisa Moylett and Zoe Apostolides, who helped to develop the proposal for this book and others before it.

I took helpful feedback on the text from my longtime friends Davy Adams and Alan Morton.

Greatest thanks of all to my wife Maureen Boyle who, being a writer herself, understands a partner having to disappear into his study for whole days.

Index

A Note About the Author

Malachi O'Doherty is a writer and broadcaster based in Belfast. He is a regular contributor to the *Belfast Telegraph* and to several BBC radio programmes. He covered the Troubles and the peace process as a journalist and has written for a number of Irish and British newspapers and magazines, including the *Irish Times, New Statesman, Scotsman* and *Guardian*.